ARAFAT AND THE PALESTINE LIBERATION ORGANIZATION

Also by Diana Reische

FOUNDING THE AMERICAN COLONIES

PATRICK HENRY

DIANA REISCHE

ARAFAT

AND THE
PALESTINE LIBERATION ORGANIZATION

FRANKLIN WATTS
NEW YORK / LONDON / TORONTO / SYDNEY / 1991

Photographs courtesy of: Wide World Photos: pp. 19, 85, 99, 112;
Magnum Photos: pp. 21 (Abbas), 79 (Bruno Barbey);
UPI/Bettmann Newsphotos: pp. 22, 40, 45, 74, 77, 86, 96, 138;
Gamma-Liaison: pp. 61 (Depardon), 123 (El Tayeb), 154 (Nabil);
Impact Visuals: p. 129 (Neal Cassidy).

Library of Congress Cataloging-in-Publication Data

Reische, Diana L.
Arafat and the Palestine Liberation Organization / by Diana Reische.
p.   cm.
Includes bibliographical references and index.
Summary: Examines the life and career of Yasir Arafat and his
leadership of the Palestinian Liberation Organization and outlines
the history of the Arab-Israeli struggle.
ISBN 0-531-11000-1
1. Arafat, Yasir, 1929–   . 2. Palestinian Arabs—Biography.
3. Munazzamat al-Taḥrīr al-Filasṭīnīyah.   4. Jewish-Arab relations.
5. Israel-Arab conflicts.   [1. Arafat, Yasir, 1929—
2. Palestinian Arabs—Biography.   3. Jewish-Arab relations.]
I. Title.
DS119.7.A6785R45   1991
322.4′092—dc20
[B]
[92]   90-46868 CIP AC

CONTENTS

ARAFAT AND THE PALESTINE LIBERATION ORGANIZATION

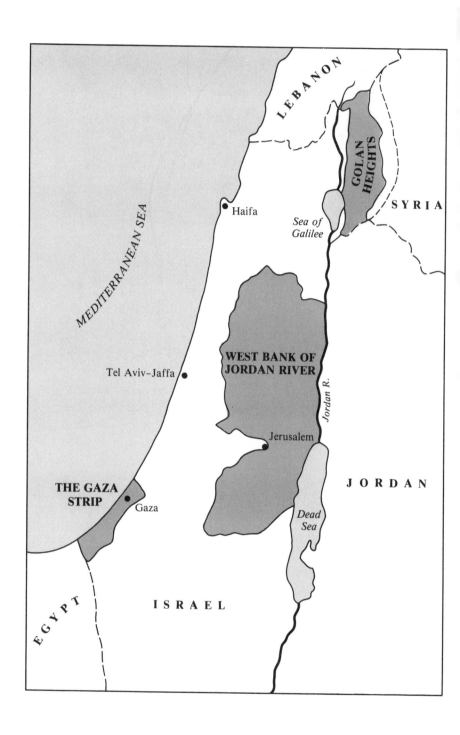

LEBANON

GOLAN HEIGHTS

SYRIA

Haifa

Sea of Galilee

MEDITERRANEAN SEA

WEST BANK OF JORDAN RIVER

Jordan R.

Tel Aviv–Jaffa

Jerusalem

JORDAN

THE GAZA STRIP

Gaza

Dead Sea

EGYPT

ISRAEL

TWO FACES OF THE "OLD MAN"

Two conflicting images of the same person:

- A cartoon shows his whiskered face beaming at Saddam Hussein, president of Iraq, and Muammar Qadaffi of Libya, as all three wave curved swords aloft. The Herblock cartoon, "The Three Musketerrorists," appeared after Iraq invaded Kuwait in 1990.
- A dignified photograph of the same face holds a place of honor in the living room of a young rebel who considers the man in the picture to be the head of his country—a country that does not exist.

These contradictory views of the same man—one scornful and contemptuously hostile, the other awash with admiration and respect—reflect the fierce debates that swirl around the Arab leader known as Yasir Arafat. He heads one of the most controversial groups in the world, the Palestine Liberation Organization, or PLO. The PLO and the Palestinians it represents are explosive fuses in the tinderbox of the Middle East. Neither Arafat nor the quarrelsome organization he heads can be safely ignored by outsiders—no matter how much they might wish to do so.

Who is this man in the checkered headdress? Is he a murdering terrorist, the world-class villain he is sometimes called? Is he a surefooted leader and wily planner who managed against great odds to unite the scattered Palestinian people, and who therefore has the clear right to speak for them? Or is Arafat an outdated figurehead scurrying around the world making speeches while events have bypassed him in a new Middle East not of his making? The answer may be all of the above or none of the above, depending on one's point of view.

To begin to understand either Arafat or the Palestine Liberation Organization he heads, it helps to enter the lives of the people for whom they speak. Without an understanding of some fraction of their pain and rage, both the man and the PLO make no sense at all.

Ala Jaroub, a thirteen-year-old in the hilltop village of Beita, shows a visitor the handmade blue nylon slingshot he keeps in a cabinet in the family's living room. Like other village youths, Ala practices with his slingshot daily, hoping for a chance to hurl a stone at the Israelis who occupy his village in what was once part of Jordan. Ala and other Beita youths see themselves as frontline fighters in a struggle to throw off Israeli control and create a state for the scattered Palestinian people.

Ala and thousands of other Palestinian youths are part of an uprising against Israeli occupation that erupted in December 1987. Known by its Arabic name, Intifada, or "throwing off," the uprising spread like water from a burst pipe through towns, villages, and refugee camps in lands occupied by Israel. Youths and men armed with rocks and Molotov cocktails (homemade gasoline bombs) hurled them at Israeli soldiers sent to keep order. Girls watched from windows to signal when troops were coming, knowing that Israeli soldiers had orders not to fire at women or children.

Since it erupted in 1987, the Intifada has drawn renewed attention to the passionate claims of two peoples—Israeli Jews and Palestinians—to the same patch of arid, contested land. The uprising opened new, festering wounds in the deadly struggle between Israelis and Arabs, who have fought five wars since 1947 to support their rival claims. The Intifada raised to a white heat the always-smoldering hatreds and political passions in the Middle East.

The unplanned uprising caught Arafat and other exiled leaders of the Palestinian movement by surprise. Since the revolt began, those long-distance leaders have scrambled to at least seem as if they are directing the struggle. Though the Intifada began spontaneously, it was molded into a loose, village-by-village organization within weeks. Money flowed in to provide food, clothing, medical care for wounded Palestinians, and pensions for widows. Pamphlets appeared with reports of events in other areas, instructions for more demonstrations and strikes, and warnings not to shoot to kill Israelis.

Behind the pamphlets and the secret committee that tries to direct the rebellion is the PLO, which most Palestinians consider to be their true government. Yet to many in the Western world, the PLO's record of terror makes it unfit for the family of civilized nations.

Such doubts do not trouble the young rebels of the Intifada. A color photograph of Arafat decorates the cabinet where Ala Jaroub keeps his slingshot. Though the PLO is banned in Israel and Israeli-occupied territories, pictures of Arafat and the PLO flag appear defiantly in villages like Beita. To the Jaroub family and many other Palestinians, Arafat and the PLO symbolize their passionate hope for a state of their own.

Like Ala Jaroub, many of the "children of stones" who keep the Intifada simmering despite the danger of death, injury, or jail have spent their entire lives under Israeli rule. The Jaroubs live in the West Bank, territory captured from Jordan by Israel in the Six Day War of 1967. The West Bank is not officially part of Israel, but every year more Israelis settle there, raising Arab fears that Israel might annex the terrority. Ironically, if Arab leaders had been willing in 1947 to accept Israel's right to exist, the West Bank might now be part of the Palestinian state dreamed of by youths such as Ala.

The rebels in the Intifada are only part of the scattered people who consider themselves Palestinians. Many Palestinian children and adults have never set foot in Palestine (modern Israel and Jordan). Their families have lived as refugees for more than forty years, nursing their grievances and dreaming of a return to that part of Palestine that has become the state of Israel. Most Arab countries have refused to give these Palestinians citizenship, so they live as stateless people with no passports. Only in Jordan and Israel itself do Palestinians live in the ancient land of Palestine.

The map on page 13 shows where the 5 million Palestinians live today. The maps on page 14 show how the region's political boundaries have shifted since 1947 as a result of Arab-Israeli wars. These wars have left the Palestinians an embittered people without a country, a people scattered throughout the world.

"We have all grown up and lived not only in diverse locales in the Arab world, but also in Western and Eastern Europe, in North and South America, in Africa and the Far East," writes Palestinian poet and political activist Fawaz Turki. "Yet we have managed to keep our

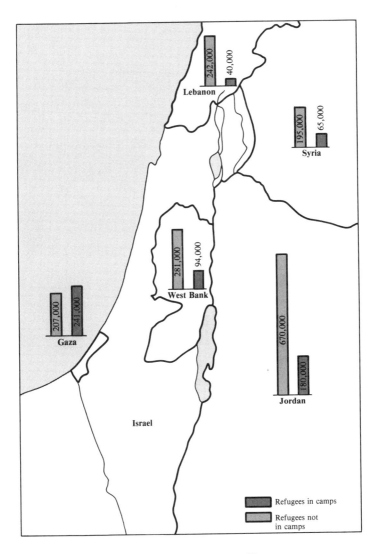

Where Palestinians live
(1988 United Nations figures)
Other Palestinians live elsewhere;
for instance, in Egypt.
This map shows the greatest concentrations.
(Kuwait, for example, had 400,000 Palestinians
before the Iraqi invasion.)

HOW THE LINES
HAVE CHANGED

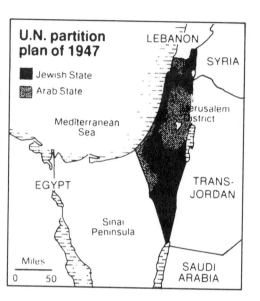

U.N. partition plan of 1947

■ Jewish State
▨ Arab State

LEBANON
SYRIA

Mediterranean Sea

Jerusalem District

EGYPT

TRANS-JORDAN

Sinai Peninsula

Miles
0   50

SAUDI ARABIA

Israel after 1948-49 war

LEBANON
SY

Mediterranean Sea

Jerusale

EGYPT

TRAN JORD

Sinai Peninsula

Miles
0   50

SAUDI ARABIA

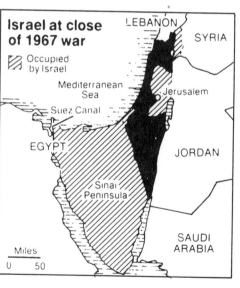

Israel at close of 1967 war

LEBANON
SYRIA

▨ Occupied by Israel

Mediterranean Sea

Suez Canal

Jerusalem

EGYPT

JORDAN

Sinai Peninsula

Miles
0   50

SAUDI ARABIA

Israel today

LEBANON
SY

Israeli Security Zone

Mediterranean Sea

Jerusalem

Gaza Strip

Gola Heigh (anne by Isra

West Bank

EGYPT

JORDA

Sinai Peninsula

Miles
0   50

SAUDI ARABIA

communal sense of national reference bounding and rebounding among us, like jugglers' weights, from year to year, from place to place, from generation to generation. . . ."[1]

Yasir Arafat, the chief spokesman for these far-flung people, is one of the world's most controversial people. Viewed by many Westerners as a terrorist, Arafat is revered by most Palestinians as their true spokesman and most effective rallying symbol. Again and again Arafat and the PLO have seemed to be totally defeated, overrun by events and left in the dust by the stampede of history. Yet again and again the man and the organization have revived and rebounded to become even stronger voices on behalf of the Palestinians.

Most outside commentators think Arafat guessed wrong when he immediately lined up with Iraq after Saddam Hussein invaded Kuwait in 1990. Arafat's decision created deep splits in the already divided leadership of the PLO. Radical elements sided with Iraq, while more cautious voices in the PLO warned that Arafat was destroying the organization by seeming to accept the takeover of one Arab country (and a major PLO financial backer) by a powerful neighbor. The decision to side with Iraq may also have shut off the flow of money from Saudi Arabia and other oil-rich countries to the PLO. Many commentators argued that Arafat's backing of Iraq had undone most of the gains achieved by the PLO in the previous ten years.

The countries of the Arab world recognize the PLO as the sole legitimate representative of the Palestinian people, although no elections have been held to verify the claim. There is no way to understand the simmering politics of the explosive Middle East without recognizing the hold Arafat and the PLO have on the imaginations of the 5 million Palestinians.

■ 15

MOBILE LEADERSHIP OF A
SCATTERED PEOPLE

As he scrambles to keep his leadership and win gains for Palestinians, Arafat faces an unusual problem. He cannot meet directly with many of his followers. Known leaders of the PLO cannot enter Israeli-run lands, yet through modern telecommunications, Arafat stays in direct contact with the secret group coordinating the Intifada in villages like Beita. The contents of pamphlets handed out in occupied territories are cleared with PLO headquarters in Tunisia, some 2,000 miles (3,200 km) from the Israeli-occupied territories, then beamed by satellite to Palestine. The materials reach Intifada street fighters through a complicated secret network. Those on the street often ignore the advice in the leaflets, yet they count on the PLO for funds and supplies to keep their protest alive.

On a typical day, aboard a jet somewhere over the Middle East, the short, paunchy man in neatly pressed battle fatigues who heads the PLO works his way swiftly through folders of papers. Many of the papers are faxes, sheets of facsimile printouts seemingly magically produced in his airborne office by mobile facsimile machines and telephones. Through the wonders of satellite communications, a man who cannot legally enter Israeli-occupied territories stays in daily, even hourly, contact with those on the ground. Arafat claims that the PLO can relay commands to troops in the field with no more than a five-minute delay.

The organization is a loose and unstable coalition of eight armed fighting forces—each with its own leaders and its own ideas about how to proceed—plus a network of social agencies serving Palestinians. As Arafat dashes around the world, raising money for the organization, persuading, arguing, and endlessly talking to scores of people, he is running what he considers to be a government in exile. Arafat says that although he is not a chief of state, he has to work twice as hard as one because he is not only supervising a bureaucracy but also running a revolution.[2] Arafat is quick to note that the PLO is not only an organization of armed fighters; it also operates hospitals and schools as part of a network of social services for the 5 million Palestinians scattered throughout the Middle East, many of them in refugee camps.

A SYMBOL IN NONSTOP MOTION

For Arafat, it is a restless, nonstop exile. He moves constantly, visiting heads of state in the twenty-two nations of the Arab world, from the Middle East to North Africa. From these countries has come most of the money to operate the PLO, a budget of at least $200 million a year, probably much more. Additional funds and support have come from communist and revolutionary governments around the world.

Arafat infuriated his biggest financial backers in 1990, when he openly sided with Iraq's invasion of Kuwait. In the ten years prior to 1990, the PLO got an estimated $10 billion from Kuwait, Saudi Arabia, and the tiny oil-rich countries known as the United Arab Emirates. The Saudis alone are said to have been giving the PLO $6 million a month before the invasion. After Arafat failed to condemn the Iraqi invasion, the little Persian Gulf emirate of Qatar began expelling Palestinians, including several PLO officials. Other reprisals were expected to follow.

Arafat also counts on Arab states to loan him the several jets that whisk him from place to place. His journeys are always secret, and often take place at night.

Arafat has no home or permanent office, though the

PLO has offices in Tunis, Tunisia, and heavily guarded compounds in Aden, Yemen, and in Baghdad, Iraq. By staying on the move, by shifting locations with no advance warning, Arafat has eluded fifty or more attempts to assassinate or ambush him. He rarely sleeps in the same place twice. As he flies around the globe, Arafat's own pilot travels as an armed passenger, ready to grab the controls in an emergency. By changing planes frequently, Arafat hopes to avoid being spotted and forced down by Israeli jets. His top aide and close friend, Khalil al-Wazir, was assassinated in 1988 by what most observers believe was an Israeli hit squad.

Yet Arafat's enemies are not limited to Israelis; they include people who are deadly enemies of one another. He has been targeted for assassination by a number of Arab terrorists who think he is too soft and flexible toward Israel.

Despite a legion of enemies, Arafat moves freely among large crowds of Palestinians in refugee camps in countries near Israel. His popularity among them so far has kept him safe. Fawaz Turki has written that Palestinians rally around Arafat because he strikes a chord in their collective soul. "He is the essential Palestinian Everyman, living a more authentically Palestinian lifestyle than any of them—no family, no home, no passport, no country, no property, consumed by Palestine and nothing else."[3] He has also been called part symbol, part actor, part statesman, part charlatan.

Arafat's admirers also say that he has *baraka,* Arabic for the divine blessing of good luck and power. His luck has saved him again and again during a life that spans more than sixty years of almost constant war and tumult over the land Arabs call Palestine. Defeated repeatedly, Arafat has engineered one comeback after another for both himself and the PLO.

To some people, Arafat is a genuine hero.
He listens here to two Palestinian women
in Lebanon as they tell him about the damage
done to their homes during an Israeli raid.

A MAN WHO INVENTED HIMSELF

Yasir Arafat has no immediate family, no personal life outside the PLO. The organization and its goals obsess him twenty-four hours a day. His stamina is legendary, driving him through eighteen-hour days of nonstop motion. Arafat wears out aides; they work in shifts to keep up with him. He does not smoke or drink, but he doesn't mind sitting in a smoke-filled room while others puff away. His only luxury seems to be stirring extra honey into his tea. His favorite snack is a gruel of cornflakes moistened with tea and sweetened with honey. Though he made a small fortune in the 1950s, Arafat has few personal possessions. He seems to have poured all his funds into building the PLO. He has no hobbies, though in rare moments of relaxation he likes to watch cartoons, particularly Tom and Jerry, Roadrunner, and Bugs Bunny.

An emotional, secretive man, Yasir Arafat has deliberately blurred the facts of his personal history. He sees himself as the living symbol of Palestinian dreams and as such, not bound by mere facts about dreary details such as where he was born, exactly who his relatives are, or what he was doing at a precise time. A symbol should be mythic, and to polish up the myth, one may improve on the facts. Arafat generally refuses to answer direct questions about himself, and he turns away inquiries into his private past. Not surprisingly, the handful of biographies about him conflict on many key details of his life.

Back in the 1960s, he remarked that he was not born until he became Abu Ammar, his *nom de guerre,* or fictitious war name. Arafat's "war name" translates roughly into "the Building Father." His admirers also call him the Old Man, a term of affection and respect.

Very little is known about Arafat's personal life and habits. In this photograph, he is caught in a rare private moment at the residence of the PLO ambassador to Tunisia.

Though his leadership has been challenged often, Arafat has confounded rivals again and again to emerge as the strongest voice and most durable leader of the loose and volatile coalition that is the PLO. Whether his leadership can survive the twin pressures of the Intifada and the tumult caused by Iraq's invasion of Kuwait is an open question.

HAS TIME RUN OUT FOR ARAFAT?

Since the Intifada exploded without direction from the PLO's distant leaders, Arafat and his associates have hustled to gain control of the angry young men and women defying Israeli authority. Many street fighters in the Intifada reject PLO advice to use caution, to move slowly, and to have patience. Many of the young people hurling stones and gasoline bombs at Israeli soldiers and settlers are even younger than Arafat was when he first committed himself to regaining Palestine for the Arabs.

Many observers think time is running out for Arafat and other graying leaders of the PLO. Other, more violent groups are challenging Fatah—Arafat's power base in the PLO—and the PLO itself for leadership of the uprising and of the Palestinian people. After Iraq invaded Kuwait in 1990, large numbers of Palestinians hailed Saddam Hussein as their new hero. Pictures of the Iraqi president sprouted alongside, and sometimes in place of, photos of Arafat. Youths in the West Bank celebrated the Iraqi invasion by taunting Israeli patrols

The PLO chairman ponders a move during
a game of chess with a colleague.

■ 23

with chants, "Saddam is coming! He's on his way! He's on his way! Saddam is going to sweep you away."

As fragile Arab unity shattered into new lineups over Kuwait, Arafat's mantle of leadership seemed more slippery than ever. Time worked against him as younger, more violent voices jockeyed to replace him as spokesman for the Palestinians. If Arafat cannot produce some results soon, other possibly more militant and violent leaders may wrest leadership of the Palestinians from him and other more cautious forces in the PLO.

Arafat was sixty years old in December 1989, when the Intifada entered its third year. He was eighteen in 1947 when the United Nations voted to partition, or divide up, Palestine to create the new state of Israel and a Palestinian state. He was nineteen in 1948 when Arabs went to war to prevent the establishment of a Jewish state and thus lost the first chance to create a state of Palestine. In the war's aftermath, hundreds of thousands of Palestinians became exiles. Arafat has spent most of the years since trying to eliminate the state of Israel and create in its place a Palestinian state. He may or may not have abandoned the first goal, but he remains passionately committed to creating a country called Palestine.

Looking at photos of Arafat, it is hard to imagine him as anyone's hero. He certainly does not look the part. Short—about 5 feet 4 or 5 inches (162.5–165 cm)—with a scraggly beard that seems never to grow or fill out, he has bulging eyes and a heavy lower lip. Under the kaffiyeh, the traditional checkered Arab scarf he wears on his head, Arafat is bald except for a fringe of graying hair.

"Palestinians are a messy and uneven people," explains Edward Said, a Palestinian-born professor of English at Columbia University. ". . . Arafat—stubbly face; small, slightly overweight body; overarticulate eloquence and all—has led and represented us for so long because he has never lost touch with what we are. Today he is the only Arab leader who needs no guards when he is among his people. He is also a great original."[4]

From the time he was a college student, Arafat outworked, outtalked, and outorganized the many others who sought to speak for Palestinians. From his days as a student leader in Egypt, he has worked harder, longer, and more effectively than anyone else to bind scattered Palestinians together in a shared sense of national identity. Arafat works eighteen- and nineteen-hour days, seven days a week, and says he never takes a day off. A guerrilla and revolutionary since his early teens, he has spent his entire life in the cause of Palestinian self-determination.

A HERO OR A COMMON TERRORIST?

One biographer of Arafat, Alan Hart, subtitled his book *Terrorist or Peacemaker?* The question is almost impossible for an outsider to answer fairly, partly because of the secrecy with which Arafat surrounds himself. He was, without question, a terrorist in his younger years. Whether he has in fact abandoned terror as a weapon or has only pretended to do so for tactical reasons is a hotly argued issue.

Both the man and the PLO are not just controversial; they are explosively controversial. People have no mild opinions about Arafat; they either loathe him or admire him. There seems to be no middle ground. A hero and symbol of their dreams to most Palestinians, he is dismissed as a common terrorist murderer by the Israeli government, which has called him the head of an organization of murderers. In 1989, a prominent member of

■ 25

the Israeli government, Ariel Sharon, called Arafat "killer Number 1," and urged his "removal." The United States government identifies Arafat as a terrorist, and because of this label denied him permission in both 1988 and 1990 to enter this country to speak to the United Nations.

Former U.S. president Jimmy Carter, who brought Israel and Egypt together for Middle East peace talks in the 1970s, described Arafat in somewhat milder terms. After being chosen to head the PLO, "Arafat was able to constrain some of the more radical terrorist groups among the Palestinians,"[5] according to President Carter. Professor Said, a leading U.S. expert on Palestinians, and a member of the PLO legislature, considers Arafat a moderating influence among Palestinians. Less admiring observers say the man is a chameleon, an opportunist who is too slippery to pin down on any important issue, and who will use any method to achieve his ends.

The organization Arafat heads provokes similar passions. One chronicler of the PLO, Jillian Becker, described its history as "full of cruelty, wretchedness, atrocity, violent death and the destruction of a country [Lebanon]. . . ."[6] By a vote of 97–1, the U.S. Senate in 1989 voted to forbid official U.S. talks with any PLO representative known to have committed terrorist acts against U.S. citizens, and to limit official contacts with the PLO. The only "no" vote was from a senator who wanted a stronger ban.

Whether Arafat is able, or even willing, to be a force for moderation in the 1990s is another difficult question for an unbiased outsider to answer. The Intifada and the Iraqi invasion of Kuwait have created intense new pressures on the PLO to produce some real gains for Palestinians. Israel celebrated its fortieth anniversary during the first year of the uprising. During those forty years, Israel became a sophisticated military power that repeatedly showed its ability to crush Arab attacks. After years of vowing to destroy Israel, the PLO now offers to negotiate. However, the Israeli government has refused to negotiate with or even officially talk to any PLO representative. One well-known Israeli radio personality was sentenced to jail in 1989 just for meeting with Arafat. That same year a minister in the Israeli government lost his post for meeting with PLO representatives.

Twenty-one of the twenty-two Arab nations refuse to recognize Israel's right to exist. (Egypt is the one Arab state that does recognize Israel.) All of them declare the PLO to be the only legitimate representative of the 5 million Palestinians. By 1990, nearly 100 countries had diplomatic relations with the PLO. The United Nations has granted the organization observer status, allowing PLO representatives to sit in but not vote on issues.

Is the PLO therefore on its way to becoming a respectable government that could take its place among the world's nations? Is it rather a cluster of terrorists nursing impossible fantasies of wiping Israel off the map? Or is it something in between? Such questions arouse passionate debate—and more questions.

DID THE PLO RENOUNCE TERROR?

After years of dodging the issue and making statements that could be interpreted in several ways, in 1988 Arafat took an enormous step for an Arab leader. In Geneva, he announced that the PLO would accept the right of Israel to exist. Arafat also said that the PLO renounced terrorism. For these two statements, Arafat earned praise from governments and commentators outside the Middle East. However, he also drew the outrage of Palestinian militants who want an all-out struggle against Israel, including terrorist bombings and any other method of destruction against soldiers and civilians alike. Several hardliners vowed to murder Arafat for daring to offer peace to Israel, while others demanded that he be replaced as PLO chairman—replaced by someone who still wants to fight.

Although Arafat acknowledged Israel's right to live in peace with its neighbors, he failed to mention that the PLO covenant, which calls for the destruction of the state of Israel, remains unchanged. Adopted in 1968, the covenant is the basic document of the PLO (see Appendix). Repeated questions about this omission are waved aside as unimportant by Arafat. Many people therefore doubt that Arafat has been speaking honestly either about giving up terrorism or accepting Israel's right to live in peace with its Arab neighbors. They believe that both he and the PLO still seek to destroy Israel. *Newsweek* magazine commented at the time of the 1988 announcement that Arafat and his confederates "have raised double-talk to an art form."[7]

Equally important has been Arafat's inability (or unwillingness) to control branches of the PLO that are still sending terrorist raids into Israel. President George Bush broke off talks with the PLO in 1990 after a group that is part of the PLO landed seaborne terrorists on a popular Israeli beach. Israeli security forces caught the terrorists before they did any harm, but the raid achieved the real objective of the Palestinian hard-liners. It caused a breakdown in the delicate and infinitely difficult efforts to get peace talks started in the Middle East.

A few months later, Iraq's invasion of Kuwait created vast new uncertainties in the shifting sands of Arab power politics. As military forces of the United States and the United Nations poured into Saudi Arabia to block further Iraqi advances, the PLO split into quarreling factions over how to react to the totally new situation.

Amid such controversies, Yasir Arafat continues his nonstop travels, his single-minded drive to create a state of Palestine. He and his top aides in the PLO know they must take new risks to stay ahead of the generation of angry young men and women hurling stones and homemade bombs in the Intifada. Militant Palestinian splinter groups say that Arafat and Fatah have become too tame and too willing to compromise; they work to sabotage Arafat's efforts. These militants use terrorism against Israel, knowing that Israel will send troops to punish the loss of Israeli lives. In so doing, the Arab hard-liners hope to discredit the efforts of the more flexible voices in the PLO. Several moderate PLO voices have also been stilled permanently. Palestinian terrorists have murdered several top PLO diplomats whom they considered too willing to compromise.

So far, Arafat has been cunning enough, lucky enough, and resilient enough to survive crushing defeats and seemingly hopeless odds against him and his cause. For more than twenty years, Arafat has dominated the PLO. The history of the Palestine Liberation Organization and Arafat's own life story intertwine. The man has no life outside the PLO. The PLO *is* his life.

CHAPTER 1

A FAMILY OF ARAB NATIONALISTS (1929–48)

Reach back in time to the years before oil pumped unimaginable wealth into the Middle East, a time between two world wars, when European colonial powers controlled the region, and Arabs plotted to win independence. England held Palestine, an ancient region on the eastern Mediterranean that has been a crossroads of history and peoples for several thousand years.

The Palestinian family into which Yasir Arafat was born on August 24, 1929, was deeply involved in Arab nationalist efforts to drive the English out of the Middle East and form an Arab state. Where was the family's sixth child born? Even so simple a question lacks a simple answer. Solid, provable facts about Yasir Arafat's personal life are as rare as whooping cranes. He probably was born in Cairo, Egypt, where his father had moved to start a new business. However, Arafat claims to have been born in Jerusalem, in a house that has since been destroyed by Israelis. Having been born in Jerusalem would make him a born Palestinian, far more suitable for a symbol of Palestinian hopes than someone born in Egypt.

The family named their third son Rahman; Yasir is a nickname he picked up later—exactly when and how is also in dispute. Yasir means easygoing, or "no problem." Arafat is not the family name, but rather one of his given names. Arafat is the name of a mountain sacred to Muslims, again a symbol suitable for an Arab leader.

Arafat's father, Abdul Rauf al-Qudwa, came from a family of merchants in Gaza, near the Mediterranean in southern Palestine. A year or two before Rahman was born, his father had sold his Gaza property and moved to Cairo. By one account, Abdul Rauf was driven out by angry Arabs for selling goods to Jewish families. Like most tales of Arafat's family and early years, the story may or may not be true.

The boy's mother came from one of Jerusalem's most prominent families, a branch of the al-Husseinis. They claim direct descent from Fatima, daughter of Muhammad, the founder of the religion known as Islam. For generations, Husseinis held the highest religious and civic posts in Jerusalem. In the fifty years before World War II, six of Jerusalem's mayors were al-Husseinis.

Yasir Arafat will not talk about his childhood, except to admit that his early years were unhappy. However, his sisters and brothers have filled in some of the blanks about his early years. After his mother died of a kidney ailment when he was four, Yasir and a younger brother were sent by Abdul Rauf to live with an uncle in Jerusalem for four years. During these years, Arafat's father often traveled to Jerusalem on business.

Abdul Rauf married a second time when Yasir was eight, and Yasir and his younger brother returned to live in the family home in Cairo. Behaving like the cruel stepmother of fairy tales, the new wife tormented Yasir and the other children. Noisy quarrels and the children's complaints caused Abdul Rauf to divorce her within a few months. However, she left deep emotional scars on Yasir. For at least twenty years afterward, he nursed a profound dislike for women in general.

His father remarried quickly, but settled this third wife into separate quarters and told Yasir's oldest sister, Inam, that she was responsible for the younger children. Inam did her best to control young Rahman/Yasir, but has admitted that she usually failed.

By the time he was ten years old, at the start of World War II, the boy was out in the streets, drilling other youths to become soldiers and Arab guerrilla fighters. Yasir had soaked up dreams of Arab nationalism from his father and others. Throughout the 1930s, Arafat's relatives plotted strikes and guerrilla attacks against English colonial rule. Like many other Arabs, they also brooded over the rising number of Jewish newcomers to Palestine.

ARAB NATIONALISM COLLIDES WITH ZIONISM

In 1880, fewer than 12,000 Jews lived in Palestine, but by 1914, the number had risen to 80,000, with more arriving every year. Many arrived with financing from Zionist organizations, groups dedicated to creating a new Jewish homeland in lands their ancestors, the Hebrews, had occupied for many centuries in biblical times. Zionists hoped to make Jerusalem the capital of a new Zion, or Jewish homeland. After Adolf Hitler's Nazi Party took power in Germany in 1933, Jewish emigration to Palestine rose sharply as Jews sought a refuge from Hitler's anti-Jewish policies. The flood of well-educated

European Jews, however, roused Arab fears of being crowded out of their homeland.

While Yasir Arafat was growing up, his mother's relative, Haj Amin al-Husseini, served as the Mufti, or head of Jerusalem's Muslim community, and unofficial mayor under English colonial rule. The Mufti was the most infamous Arab nationalist of his time. Much of the subsequent tragedy of the Palestinian people stems from his violent rabble-rousing, from his fanatical hatred of the Jewish people, and from his total refusal to compromise. The Mufti saw Jewish immigration as a direct threat to his dream of creating an Arab nation once the English were driven out. He deliberately fanned Arab fears of being displaced by Jews, and encouraged murderous attacks on Jewish settlers. The terrorist group Black Hand, which was behind many anti-Jewish attacks, took oaths to die for the Mufti.

In 1929, the year Arafat was born, followers of Haj Amin murdered a hundred Jews in three communities. During the four years that Yasir lived in Jerusalem after his mother's death, the Mufti thundered that selling land to Jews was a crime against Allah (the Muslim name for God). He encouraged his followers to beat up Arab landowners who sold to Jews, and to smash their property. He called for "holy assassins" to murder people who opposed such ideas.

Yasir was six when the Mufti sponsored a Palestinian Arab Party inspired by Germany's Nazi Party. A year later, in 1936, the Mufti called a general strike to stop further Jewish immigration. The strike lasted eight months and brought most of the area's business to a standstill.

Yasir's father was in Jerusalem on business during the general strike and got caught up in the anti-Jewish frenzy. Abdul Rauf belonged to a shadowy radical group

■ 33

known as the Muslim Brotherhood, which promoted ties between Muslims in various Arab countries and plotted a return to a simpler, more fundamental form of Islam that rejected Western influences. The Brotherhood also hoped to launch a "holy war" of armed revolution against the British occupying army. To promote its plans, the Brotherhood used kidnapping, assassinations, and other violent means to terrify or eliminate opponents.

By the time Abdul Rauf brought his eight-year-old son, Yasir, back to Cairo, he was deep in Brotherhood plots and intrigues and paid little attention to the chubby, silent boy.

THE MURDER OF A TEACHER

Yasir's sister Inam did her best to control the stubborn little boy, but Yasir usually ignored her. He was so withdrawn and silent that some visitors suggested he might be retarded. Apparently, he was just bored. When he found a person to admire, he began to show unexpected talents.

As was common for Muslim boys of his age, Arafat was sent to religion classes every day with a Muslim scholar. His teacher was an uncle of his mother's, Yusef al-Akbar. The uncle discovered that Yasir learned with amazing speed. He could repeat whole passages after seeing them once. The old scholar interpreted Yasir's photographic memory as a sign from Allah that Yasir was marked for greatness. The old man insisted to Yasir's father that because of these gifts from Allah, the family must treat the boy with great respect.

Basking in such praise, Yasir happily stayed long after regular classes, soaking up the old man's teachings. In addition to lessons about Islam, Yusef told Yasir endless stories about his mother's family. He described the al-Husseinis as far grander and more distinguished than Abdul Rauf's family of merchants.

Dazzled by the image of himself as marked for glory by Allah, Yasir became insufferable at home. He flaunted a contempt for his father and openly disobeyed him. The hot-tempered Abdul Rauf beat the boy regularly, but Yasir continued to be sullen, disobedient, and arrogant.

Yasir's brother Zaeed told Arafat biographer Thomas Kiernan that his father went to the old man and swore to kill him if he didn't stop brainwashing the boy. Soon, however, Yusef was again telling Yasir such stories as how his father had been driven out of Gaza because of his dealings with Zionist Jews. The predictable explosion came after Yasir refused to obey his oldest brother, whom his father had left in charge. After a family fight, Yasir fled to his uncle's house, where his father found him clinging to Yusef's robes. Yasir pleaded with his father to let him live with the old man.

According to Kiernan's account, the next morning Yusef was found dead. He had been garroted, strangled with a cord, and his body was left hanging. This was the trademark assassination method of the Muslim Brotherhood. During an investigation into the death, the policeman in charge of the questioning was also murdered.

Not long afterward, in 1939, Abdul Rauf moved the family back to Gaza, perhaps to avoid questions about the murders. In Gaza, he became even more active in the Muslim Brotherhood and other secret groups that were hatching plots to drive the British from Palestine.

A TEENAGE RECRUIT

During Yasir's early teens in Gaza, Great Britain was struggling desperately against Nazi Germany in World War II. Some Arab nationalists—including Yasir's family—saw the war as a chance to break free of British colonial rule. They therefore sided with the Nazis against Britain and the Allies. The Mufti, for instance, spent the war in Nazi Germany, passing spy information to the Nazis from his contacts in the Middle East.

Plots and plans swirled through Palestine, stirring dreams of heroic adventure in young Yasir. His sister Inam did her best to control Yasir and see that he went to school, but more and more often he roamed the streets, off on secret doings of his own. A classmate described him as a "fat, moody boy who managed to frighten everyone a little."[1]

In Gaza, Yasir fell under the influence of a young Lebanese math teacher, Majid Halaby. Halaby spotted Yasir as the best math student in school and gave him special attention. By some accounts, it was Halaby who nicknamed the boy Yasir. Halaby had other business in Palestine besides teaching. He had come to Gaza on secret instructions from a group of Arab nationalists. He was radioing intelligence information about the Middle East to Haj Amin's Nazi spy operation.

Halaby began to train Yasir and other boys as guerrilla fighters, using for himself the nom de guerre of Abu Khalid. For a while, Halaby lived with Yasir's family, but he had to leave after angering the boy's father and other parents. Without seeking permission from their fathers, Halaby took fifteen-year-old Yasir and other boys to Jerusalem. There they met with Abdul Khadar al-Husseini, the Mufti's nephew, a leading Arab guerrilla fighter. Al-Husseini told his young relative to go home and work under his father for the Arab nationalist cause.

Not long after the trip, Halaby was murdered. By some accounts, it was believed that Yasir's father ordered the killing. Yasir was told that his friend died heroically in a guerrilla raid. The boy vowed to carry on the work of his dead idol. Abdul Khadar al-Husseini persuaded him to do so by returning to school in Gaza and recruiting more guerrillas. Yasir quickly showed his organizational skills by recruiting more than 300 youths to a group he named in honor of his former teacher, the Martyr Abu Khalid Society.

By 1946, sixteen-year-old Yasir was smuggling weapons into Palestine from Egypt. The fact that he spoke Arabic with a Cairo accent made it easier for him to slip past British patrols than for Arabs who spoke with the distinctive Palestinian accent. It also made Arafat more effective in bargaining with Cairo dealers, who were likely to boost prices when they thought they were dealing with Palestinians.

When it became harder to buy guns in the cities, Arafat made daring trips past desert bandits to reach Bedouin tribes who could sell him guns. This gunrunning gained Arafat a reputation for courage among Palestinians and marked him as a possible leader among Arab nationalists.

TWO CLAIMS TO ONE LAND

Arab ambitions for Palestine collided with the plans of Jewish organizers to form a new Jewish state. What the Arabs called Palestine (*filastin* in Arabic), Zionists were calling Israel. Both groups cited ancient claims to the same land, and both believed that their God had chosen them as heirs to the land.

Palestine, the region both groups sought to control, is a strip of mostly arid land bounded by the Mediterranean on the west, Egypt's Sinai Peninsula on the southwest, and Syria and Lebanon on the north. It includes places sacred to three religions—Judaism, Christianity, and Islam. To many, it is not Palestine, but the Holy Land of both the Old and New Testaments. Jerusalem is considered a holy city by all three religions.

An ancient crossroads of peoples and empires, Palestine is named for the Philistines, one of the peoples who lived in the region before the Israelites conquered the area. For several hundred years, the land was a Hebrew kingdom before it was overrun by the Assyrians and Babylonians. Then the Romans conquered the region and absorbed Palestine as a province in their empire. Arab armies overran Palestine in the seventh century and converted most of the population to Islam.

Between 1516 and World War I, the Turkish Ottoman Empire ruled Palestine. The Ottoman Empire dissolved after Turkey sided with the losing side in World War I. In the scramble to divide the Middle East among the winners, Britain took Palestine in 1920 under a "mandate" from the League of Nations.

Zionists hoped that the British would yield to their dream of creating a Jewish homeland. The British prime minister in 1917 had issued a declaration promising a "national home for the Jewish people" so long as the rest of the population of Palestine was not harmed. At the time of the Balfour Declaration, about 90 percent of Palestine's population was Arab. However, since the turn of the century, Jews had been filtering back into their ancient homeland in increasing numbers. Financed partly by Zionist groups, Jewish settlers bought Arab farms and businesses in Palestine. By 1914, when World War I began, about 80,000 Jews lived in Palestine, and about 700,000 Arabs. About 90 percent of the Arabs were Muslim, the rest Christian.

To complicate matters further, the British gave two-thirds of Palestine to Abdullah Hussein, an Arab nationalist sheik who formed the new country of Transjordan. Transjordan lay east of the Jordan River, in an area that is almost all desert. Transjordan's new ruler eyed the greener lands west of the river, and plotted ways to add it to his kingdom.

It was the flow of Jewish immigrants, though, that stirred the greatest fears among Arab Palestinians. From 1920 on, explosions of Arab violence against Jewish newcomers became more frequent. After Hitler gained power in Germany in 1933, immigration to Palestine increased. By 1936, 380,000 Jews lived in Palestine, out of a total population of 1.3 million people. Rising Jewish immigration triggered a series of strikes and anti-Jewish riots between 1936 and 1939. Hoping to defuse the Arabs' anger, the British in 1939 clamped a strict immigration limit on Jews coming to Palestine, thereby sealing off the only real refuge available to most European Jews seeking to escape the Nazis. Then World War II erupted, and Jews all over the world turned their attention to backing the struggle to defeat the Nazis.

At war's end, worldwide horror at the mass murder of Jews by the Nazis gave powerful new force to Zionist demands for a state that would provide a safe haven for Jews. At the start of 1947, the Jewish population of Palestine was about 600,000, one-third of the population. Jewish settlers demanded the creation of a new Jewish state immediately, in Palestine.

THE UN PARTITION PLAN

The entire Middle East was in ferment, with a shifting lineup of groups and countries jockeying to gain control of more land. Arabs competed with Arabs as well as with Jewish settlers for control of Palestine. In 1947 the new United Nations tried to satisfy competing Arab and Jewish claims to the Holy Land by adopting a plan to partition, or divide, Palestine into two states—one Jewish, one Arab Palestinian.

Jewish groups in Palestine accepted the UN partition plan, though it offered them a chopped-up patchwork of land. The plan made Jerusalem an international zone instead of the capital of a Jewish homeland as Jews had prayed for for centuries. It did not give them as much land as they wanted, but it was better than nothing. Arab Palestinians, however, whipped into frenzies by Haj Amin, flatly rejected the UN partition. They vowed to fight to prevent any partition and to drive Israelis into the sea. They thereby lost the chance to create a state of Palestine peacefully. As the map on p. 14 shows, the West Bank—now torn by the Intifada—would have become part of the state of Palestine.

THE 1947–48 WAR AND ITS AFTERMATH

On May 14, 1948, British troops withdrew from Palestine. Zionist forces moved in behind, quickly securing key positions. Prime Minister David Ben-Gurion proclaimed the State of Israel. Even before the formal announcement, Israelis were fighting an undeclared civil war with Palestinian guerrillas. After the proclamation of Israel, armies of neighboring Arab countries moved in to join the attack on Israel.

When the war started, Arafat was a college student

British troops remove Jewish refugees from the ship Exodus *in 1947 at Haifa, after British destroyers intercepted the ship off the coast of Palestine. Masses of Jewish refugees attempted "illegal" immigration to Palestine during the period leading up to the creation of the state of Israel.*

in Cairo. He joined a Muslim Brotherhood unit that was attacking a Jewish settlement at Kfar Darome. By at least one account, nineteen-year-old Yasir was giving orders to the Egyptian volunteers.

Arabs still argue bitterly about what went wrong in 1948. Jewish forces were far better organized than the fragmented Arabs, who operated under several rival leaderships, each suspicious of the other. Whatever the cause, a vastly outnumbered Israel trounced the combined Arab armies and guerrilla forces.

Arafat told biographer Alan Hart that the Palestinians were betrayed by the Arab regimes and by the British, who worked to create a Jewish state.[2] He recalled with bitterness being forced to hand over his weapons to Egyptian troops who disarmed Palestinians.

By the time peace was reached in 1949, Israel had annexed several areas set aside by the 1947 UN partition for the Palestinian state that was never created. Israel now had not the 54 percent of Palestine given it by the UN partition plan, but 72 percent of all Palestine. Israel controlled all of the Negev region except for the Gaza Strip. By demanding *all* of Palestine, and going to war to take it, Arab leaders had in fact cost the Palestinians still more territory.

A Palestinian state could still have been formed out of the lands not yet lost to Israel. Instead, neighboring Arab nations carved off chunks for themselves. In her history of the PLO, Jillian Becker argues that if extremist Arab leaders like the Mufti had not insisted that a Palestinian state must exist *instead* of a state of Israel, a Palestinian nation could have been formed then.

Egypt claimed the region around the town of Gaza, the narrow "Gaza Strip" on the Mediterranean coast north of the Negev desert. Transjordan took control of the much larger area west of the Jordan River known as the West Bank. The West Bank includes the lands of the biblical Israelites known as Judea and Samaria. Syria took a small strategic area in the north that overlooks Galilee. Jerusalem became a divided city. Half belonged to Israel, the other half to Transjordan, which soon renamed itself Jordan, since it was now on both sides of the river.

FLIGHT OR EXPULSION?

During and after the 1948 war, some 700,000 Palestinian Arabs left their homes. Did the refugees flee or were they driven from their homeland? Most Israeli historians insist that most refugees fled in wild panic, following the orders of leaders like the Mufti who told them to get out of the way of armies, and that they could return very soon to reclaim their lands, once the Israelis had been "driven to the sea."

Many Palestinians, however, remember Israeli trucks with loudspeakers arriving in their village, giving them a few hours to evacuate. The Palestinian poet Fawaz Turki, for instance, remembers that he was eight years old when foreign voices shouted from loudspeakers, "Get your women and children out." [3] He remembers flares, smoke, and fireworks over the houses of Haifa. The next day, in panic, his family fled toward the Lebanese border to become part of the hundreds of thousands of Palestinians who would live in refugee camps.

The American journalist David Shipler, who won a Pulitzer Prize for his book *Arab and Jew: Wounded Spirits in the Promised Land,* found that people ran for a variety of reasons. Some simply fled to get out of the war zone. Some people told Shipler they had heard Arab Legion broadcasts telling them to leave, that they could return as soon as the fighting was over. Some wealthy Palestinians left on vacation, assuming they could return in a few weeks when things quieted down. Shipler also

■ 43

found that some people were deliberately and forcibly expelled by Israelis. Still others fled because they believed if Jews reached their villages, Arabs would be massacred, as had happened in the village of Deir Yassin in April of 1948.[4]

Many of those who later became top leaders in the Palestine Liberation Organization remember vividly the day they fled with their families and became refugees, people without homes. Among them was twelve-year-old Khalil al-Wazir, the son of a grocer in Ramleh. He later told of the July day in 1948 when all the men of his village gathered, saying that the Jews were going to destroy Ramleh as they had Deir Yassin. The boy and most Ramleh residents took refuge in the church. Israeli soldiers entered the church and took some of the youths away. When the villagers came out, they found bodies of men, women, and children littering the street.[5] Later that day, al-Wazir's family packed what belongings they could carry and joined the flight.

Khalad al-Hassan returned home from work one day in 1948 to find that his family had vanished from their home in Haifa. His mother had left a note saying it was better to save five people than wait for him and possibly lose all six. It took al-Hassan nearly two years to find his family. He and his brother Hani are now both top PLO diplomats.

Whatever the reasons that caused them to flee their homes, at the end of the war, 725,000 Palestinians had become refugees. Arab countries took most of them in, but did not encourage them to settle permanently or to become citizens. Instead, the Palestinians were put in temporary camps, and treated as temporary refugees who would return to their old homes soon. Instead of settling into new homes and getting on with their lives, refugees in the camps came to live in a permanent state of limbo. They also became pawns in the endless power struggles

Before the second truce in Palestine went into effect during the 1948 war, blindfolded Arabs are taken through the Jewish lines for interrogation by Jewish security.

of the Middle East, as Arab leaders vied for land and influence and the tiny state of Israel struggled to establish itself among a sea of hostile Arabs. Some 160,000 Palestinians remained within the borders of the new state of Israel and become Israeli citizens.

As hundreds of thousands of refugees sought shelter in refugee camps, Arafat's relatives suggested he head for the United States to attend college. He signed up to attend the University of Texas and applied for a U.S. visa. But in the months while he waited for permission to enter the United States, events changed his mind.

CHAPTER 2

"DON'T FORGET PALESTINE" (1949–56)

The old government had just fallen when the president of Egypt's new revolutionary government agreed in 1952 to meet with a group of students from a Cairo university. A student leader handed him a petition signed in blood and titled "Don't Forget Palestine." The petition was typical Arafat showmanship. Even as a student, he knew how to make dramatic gestures that captured the attention of important people. It was also typical that even as a student, Arafat could get an audience with the busy head of a new revolutionary government. In only a few years, Arafat had emerged from flat despair to become the leader of a new generation of Palestinians plotting to retake their homeland.

A GUERRILLA IN TRAINING

Brooding over the loss of Palestine, and at what he saw as betrayal by Arab states, Arafat in 1948 decided to leave for college in the United States. An old man who saw him then said Arafat returned from fighting in Jerusalem like a boy in mourning.[1] Months passed while he waited for a visa that would allow him to enter this country. During this time, he rethought the whole situation. "I saw a new way forward and said to myself, No, I will not leave."[2] Arafat decided instead to devote himself to regaining Palestine. He considered joining the Egyptian army, but his father urged him to go back to school.

Back in Cairo, Arafat enrolled in a technical school to complete the high school education he had quit to become a guerrilla fighter. However, Egypt was a hotbed of plots to overthrow the British and the existing government, and the school turned out to be a training ground for commandos. In school shops, the faculty demonstrated how to make bombs and other weapons. Arafat showed a real talent for the work.

In 1949 he again left Cairo when his father took a minor job with the Mufti in Egyptian-controlled Gaza. Back in Palestine after his years in Nazi Germany, the Mufti was trying to form a Palestinian government there, and Yasir and his brothers moved to Gaza to work for Haj Amin al-Husseini.

The next three years were tumultuous, as Egypt splintered into civil war. In Gaza, plots and counterplots swirled through the refugee camps that housed nearly 250,000 Palestinians. People talked excitedly about how to drive the Israelis out of Palestine and Haj Amin fanned anti-Jewish hatred. At the same time, there were thousands of Egyptians in Gaza, many of them backing one group or another in the struggle for power in Egypt. Yasir Arafat, with his uncanny skill for making friends in the right places, befriended several key officers in the army group that finally won in 1952.

Meanwhile, Yasir and his brothers worked in Gaza under their father's direction in Haj Amin's Palestinian operation. Some jobs were boring, like passing out leaflets and running errands, but the brothers also trained as terrorists. Yasir grumbled about the physical hardships, but he improved his poor marksmanship a little. He was still physically clumsy in a fight, but he could outthink and outplan the others. He ended up as squad leader.

In their first outings as Gaza guerrillas, the squad fought not Israelis, but other Palestinians. Haj Amin sent them to terrorize Palestinians in Jerusalem who had agreed to let Transjordan take over the West Bank. The Mufti told his followers that they now had two enemies: the Jews and the Jordanians.

On one raid, Arafat's squad walked into an ambush. Bruised from clubbings and bleeding from knife wounds, they escaped. One of Arafat's squad members recalled that Arafat seethed with fury as he walked over to the youth suspected (falsely, it turned out) of betraying them. He calmly put a pistol to the boy's head and shot him. Although Arafat swore his squad to secrecy, word of the murder leaked out. Hauled before the Mufti for questioning, Yasir was pardoned because of his family connections.

As feuds among the Palestinians sapped their energies for fighting Israel, Arafat lost his respect for the Mufti. He began ignoring orders. Fearing that the whole family might be punished for Yasir's attitude, his father offered to pay his expenses if he would leave Gaza to attend college.

A SECRETIVE STUDENT ACTIVIST

In August 1951, Arafat enrolled at the University of Fuad the First in Cairo, a school boiling with political ferment. The regime of a weak and corrupt king was crumbling. At the same time, Arab nationalists plotted ways to force the British from their military base at the Suez

Canal, a vital transportation link between the Red Sea and the Mediterranean.

Arafat registered as Yasir Muhammad Arafat, dropping his father's name of al-Qudwa, and keeping quiet about his al-Husseini connections. Even then, Arafat was secretive about his private life, and accounts of his college years are difficult to prove or disprove. Even close friends, however, admit that he showed an explosive temper.

According to some accounts, Arafat was engaged briefly in 1951. The young woman told biographer Thomas Kiernan that Arafat turned on her after learning that two of her friends were Jews. Two days after Arafat met the girls, their father was murdered. Kiernan reports that Arafat flew into a violent rage when his fiancée wept for her friends. She was too terrified of him to break the engagement herself, but her father cancelled the wedding when he learned Arafat's real identity.[3] Arafat has denied ever having known the young woman.

Arafat studied civil engineering, but his real interest was organizing the many Palestinians at the university. He got himself elected chairman of the Palestinian Student Federation (PSF), which until then had been mostly talk and bluster. Arafat widened its scope and reach. He convinced Egyptian authorities to let him set up a training camp on the campus, supposedly to drill students for fighting the British in Suez. He also talked the Arab League, an umbrella group of Arab nations, into giving scholarships to Palestinian students. Despite such successes, in 1953 rivals in the student organization accused Arafat of arrogance and of favoring people from Gaza over other Palestinians. They voted him out of office.

Never one to accept defeat, Arafat promptly formed a competing group, the General Union of Palestinian Students (GUPS), and built it into a new power base.

GUPS printed what was supposedly a student newspaper, *The Voice of Palestine,* and Arafat talked Egyptian authorities into allowing wide distribution of it. He recalls that it was read not only in Cairo, but in Gaza, Jordan, Syria, Iraq, Lebanon, and elsewhere. "It was our first underground way of making contact with those who could organize."[4]

The "student" newsletter was in fact a "how to" manual telling scattered Palestinians how to organize. It encouraged them to form cells, small secret units of guerrillas, to raid across the Israeli border. The *Voice* argued that when Israel inevitably struck back, Arab countries would be drawn into the struggle. Here was the tactic Arafat would use often in the PLO—promote raids into Israel as a way of forcing Arab states to come to the aid of Palestinians.

When Arafat tried to unite all Palestinian student groups into one organization in 1955, the PSF resisted. By some accounts, the Muslim Brotherhood threw its weight behind Arafat. After several PSF members were murdered, resistance to Arafat collapsed, and he was elected chairman of the combined group.

By the time he left college in 1956, Arafat had chaired student Palestinian groups for five years. He had forged working friendships with the men who later helped him found Fatah, the armed fighting group that is his power base.

SALAH KHALAF AND KHALIL AL-WAZIR

Salah Khalaf was eighteen, four years younger than Arafat, and the leader of a small guerrilla band in Gaza when he first met Arafat in 1951. A literature student whose family came from Jaffa, Khalaf showed up at the university to observe Arafat's methods for training student commandos. At the time, Arafat was also running for president of the PSF. Khalaf threw his support, and perhaps that of the Muslim Brotherhood to which he belonged, behind Arafat.

In Gaza, Khalaf had taken commando training along with Khalil al-Wazir, the third founder of Fatah. Born in Ramleh in 1935, Khalil al-Wazir was twelve when his family fled their home. The experience seared him, leaving a fierce hatred for Israel. He was eighteen when he trained in Gaza with Khalaf. Their instructor was probably an Egyptian officer who was a secret member of the Muslim Brotherhood, and one of Arafat's contacts in Cairo. Once his own training was done, al-Wazir began recruiting and training other Palestinians. Egypt did not allow Palestinians to take guerrilla courses, so it had to be done secretly. Al-Wazir told Alan Hart how it was done:

"I had to pretend that I was organizing a sports club. To get my boys fit I used to run them from Gaza to Deir El-Balah, a distance of some ten to fifteen miles. We left before it was light in the morning and we did not return until it was dark in the evening."[5] They also learned to work with explosives, mining roads and railway tracks used by Israeli patrols.

Arrested by the Egyptians for making bombs, al-Wazir sent word to Arafat, who used his contacts in the government to get al-Wazir released. The two men had not met personally as yet, but they had been in contact. After al-Wazir's release, Arafat traveled secretly to Gaza to meet him. They talked for three days, cementing a lifelong partnership.

THE GAZA RAID

Arafat and al-Wazir planned a raid on Israel's water storage facilities, hoping the attack would draw Israeli forces across the borders in response. Israel sent para-troopers into Gaza, where they hit not only Palestinian bases, but the Egyptian army headquarters. The Israeli raid humiliated the Egyptians by exposing their military weakness.

Immediately after the raid, al-Wazir rounded up Palestinians in Gaza for mass demonstrations demanding that Egypt declare war on Israel. Rioting demonstrators turned on Egyptian authorities, and burned some Egyptian offices in Gaza. In Cairo, Arafat led a demonstration at the headquarters of the Arab League. He demanded that President Gamal Abdel Nasser meet with him and other students to talk about Gaza. Nasser agreed to the meeting. However, the Gaza raid had humiliated and infuriated Nasser. It was one of several events leading to war over the Suez Canal in 1956, a war Arafat had hoped to provoke and Nasser had tried to avoid.

The Suez crisis began after Nasser seized the canal from its British and French owners and shut it to Israeli shipping. Israeli troops moved swiftly, overrunning the Sinai Peninsula and the Gaza Strip on their way to Suez. During the fighting, al-Wazir headed a Gaza underground group that included his fifteen-year-old cousin Intissar (who later became his wife). Arafat joined the Egyptian army as part of a bomb disposal squad in Port Said.

When peace was reached in 1957, Israel withdrew from Suez and the Sinai. Arafat was offered a post as an Egyptian army officer, but he had other plans.

FORGING THE PALESTINIAN NETWORK

As early as 1953, Arafat had talked of forming an independent Palestinian liberation movement, one not tied to Egypt or any Arab state. As students, he and his friends had begun building a network of Palestinian contacts in many countries. Israel's swift victory in the Suez crisis convinced them that they had no immediate hope of winning a military clash. But they continued to organize for the future.

Arafat, al-Wazir, and Khalaf went to Prague, Czechoslovakia, in 1956 for a student conference sponsored by the Soviet Union. On their way home, they stopped in Stuttgart, Germany, to meet with other Palestinian students. Some of the first talks leading to the founding of Fatah took place in Stuttgart.

That same year, Arafat was jailed in Egypt along with several hundred others after a failed attempt by the Muslim Brotherhood to assassinate Nasser. He talked himself out of jail by naming key Egyptian leaders as personal contacts. However, he realized that he was no longer quite welcome in Egypt. He had graduated from college and needed to earn a living. He applied for a job in Kuwait, where oil was just beginning to pump new wealth into desert lands.

CHAPTER 3

FATAH AND THE PLO

In 1959, the future PLO chairman sometimes could be found on the sandy streets of Kuwait in a used pickup truck bearing the sign, "The Free Palestine Construction Company, Y. Arafat, Proprietor." Kuwait was still an obscure desert sheikdom under British colonial rule, a land only beginning to tap the huge pools of oil that would transform it into an economic giant. For well-educated Palestinians, Kuwait offered great opportunities. The government was building everything from roads and housing to airports and schools. There were far more jobs than qualified workers. Palestinians could not become citizens there, but they could make plenty of money.

Arafat arrived in 1957 and took a job as an engineer in the Department of Water Supply. Within two years, he had formed his own construction company on the side. One of his first contracts was for the plumbing for a block of apartments. In his post as a government water engineer, Arafat issued his own company the permits needed. Not surprisingly, business boomed, and Arafat became a wealthy young man. As the head of a prospering business, he was able to send for his friends Khalil al-Wazir and Salah Khalaf. All of them prospered in the boomtown atmosphere of Kuwait.

By day, the old college cronies earned their livings, but every night they talked for hours with like-minded people about Palestine. Living in tents in the half-built city, they spoke endlessly of how Palestinians lived as second-class citizens, without passports, without a state of their own.

A MOVEMENT CALLED FATAH

The group of young professionals around Arafat dubbed themselves the "Generation of Revenge." An older "Generation of Disaster" had lost Palestine; the younger generation plotted to get it back and to take revenge on those who now occupied Palestine. As they talked and argued, one of the most articulate speakers to emerge was an intellectual named Khalad al-Hassan, whose family had fled from Haifa in 1948. Al-Hassan had tried to form underground Palestinian groups in Syria, but he failed, and moved to Kuwait. He urged the others to copy the techniques of modern revolutions like that of China. He argued passionately for democratic decision-making and collective, or group, leadership in any movement they formed.

A core group consisting of Arafat, al-Wazir, Khalaf, al-Hassan, and a few others formed a secret organization, probably in 1959—they disagree now on the exact year. The founders called themselves a movement, implying that their group was not closed, but open to any Palestinian. It took a while to find a name. Their early choice, the Palestinian National Liberation Movement, lacked razzle-dazzle. Using the Arabic initials, they got the words Hataf, then reversed the order into Fatah. In Arabic, Fatah means "conquest" (or "victory").

Over months of talking, Fatah's founders agreed on five central points: 1) their goal was liberating Palestine; 2) they would use armed struggle to reach that goal; 3) they would rely on Palestinians, not outsiders, for the organization needed to win; 4) they would cooperate with friendly Arab forces, and with friendly international forces; and 5) Fatah would have collective leadership, with no one person outranking the others.

In deciding to rely on Palestinians alone, Fatah swam against the mainstream of Arab thought at a time when Nasser of Egypt was promoting Arab nationalism and unity. The Fatah group believed that Palestinians should expect nothing from corrupt Arab regimes, that they must not count on or be tied to any Middle Eastern governments or political parties. The founders did, however, seek recruits and money widely. Arafat proved to be the ablest fund-raiser, tapping such sources as the Kuwaiti ruling family. He also poured his own small fortune into Fatah's efforts.

RECRUITING FEDAYEEN

Using the same technique that had worked at the university, in 1959 Fatah began publishing a magazine called *Our Palestine*. It was distributed not only in Kuwait, but in Palestinian refugee camps elsewhere. As editor, al-Wazir crammed the magazine with articles of passionate and inflammatory propaganda. The magazine called for terrorist violence against Israel. It urged Palestinians to become *fedayeen,* guerrilla fighters. The word also means "men of sacrifice" who are ready to die for a cause.

A typical article in *Our Palestine* challenged: "Where

are you, dispersed people . . . where? Are you just flotsam, just jetsam strewn around? . . . How do you live? What's become of you? Are you living with your kith and kin, or are you scattered far and wide?'' The magazine lashed out at Arab governments, who "have stopped the Palestinian mouths, turned their hands, deprived them of their freedom of action in what is left of their country, resisted the idea of their regroupment, turned them into a theatrical claque which applauds this and reviles that. . . ."[1]

While al-Wazir worked openly as a teacher and secretly as the magazine's editor, he also took charge of distributing *Our Palestine* through his underground contacts. Readers were encouraged to write Fatah through a post office box. When they did, al-Wazir or someone else slipped out of Kuwait to make contact.

Syria and Egypt promptly banned the magazine as subversive. The ban—and news that police were punishing people for reading the magazine—helped Fatah recruit more members by making the movement seem important and exciting.

THE UNDERGROUND YEARS

Al-Wazir urged recruits to form small secret cells. Just as an organic cell can split and reproduce itself, he said, a Fatah cell could give birth to more cells in a widening network. Fatah's goal was to link Palestinians everywhere, to bind them into a sense of national unity. Then they would be strong enough to challenge Israel.

Throughout the Middle East, Palestinians were forbidden to form organizations, even labor unions. For its first ten years, Fatah worked underground. These underground years cemented a habit of secrecy that makes it hard to trace exactly what happened when or who was where. Arafat, al-Wazir, and the others traveled often, raising money and recruiting in the refugee camps and Arab capitals.

Using forged passports, Arafat toured refugee camps in 1961. He said later that the experience seared his soul with the obsession to win back Palestine. Thomas Kiernan quotes him as saying he had not known before the "degradation and humiliation so many of my people were forced to endure because of the Zionists." [2]

Though it was only one of many Palestinian underground groups operating by the 1960s, Fatah had several advantages over most groups, among them the organizational skills of Arafat and al-Wazir. Fatah leaders understood the power of symbols. They adopted the kaffiyeh, the checkered scarf worn by Arab nationalist fighters in the 1930s. The scarf helped make these Fatah professionals acceptable to Palestinian peasants, or *fellahin*. To the fellahin, Fatah's message was simple and clear: Our goal is to return to Palestine. Even the most uneducated fellahin could identify with that. Unlike some groups, Fatah managed to link Palestinian intellectuals with the less educated masses in the refugee camps.

Arafat and al-Wazir were also skilled at finding useful allies. Fatah published *Our Palestine* through an influential group in Lebanon. Al-Wazir moved there to supervise publication, and he used Lebanon as his base for more organizing for Fatah. That same year, al-Wazir again met his cousin Intissar, who had been part of his guerrilla group in Gaza. He asked her if she was ready to resume their secret work, and after she agreed, he proposed marriage. Their family became the closest thing Yasir Arafat had to family life.

Fatah gained a powerful ally after Algeria won independence from France in 1962. The new government agreed to support Fatah. With government approval, Fatah opened its first official office—the Bureau de la Palestine—in Algiers with al-Wazir as manager. Any Palestinian who wanted to work in Algeria had to get a work permit from the bureau. Permits went to those who pledged part of their salary to Fatah.

The Algerian office gave Fatah an official base and a way to meet Third World leaders such as visiting Chinese communists. After making contacts in Algiers, Arafat and several others went to China seeking arms and other help. The Chinese told them Fatah could not win a revolution because it had no base among the population actually living in Palestine. The Chinese did promise to provide arms if Fatah could show a history of successful commando raids. This promise confirmed Arafat's and al-Wazir's determination to start military actions.

Meanwhile, Fatah built its numbers through another ally, the General Union of Palestinian Students, a group that grew out of the student organization Arafat had begun in Cairo. GUPS enrolled thousands of Palestinian students not only in the Arab world, but in Europe as well. Fatah had great success recruiting students in Lebanese and Algerian colleges, and among the many Palestinians in West Germany. The head of the German students, Hani al-Hassan, was a younger brother of Fatah leader Khalad al-Hassan. Hani headed GUPS worldwide, giving him access to Palestinian students wherever they lived.

Fatah was not the only underground group recruiting Palestinians. Most groups disappeared quickly, but a few grew to rival Fatah. The most important of these was the Popular Front for the Liberation of Palestine, brainchild of George Habash, a Greek Orthodox Christian who had become a hard-line Marxist, advocating social revolution as well as national liberation. A medical student at the American University in Beirut, Habash had been driven from his home in Lydda in 1948 by Israeli forces. At the Beirut university, Habash and other stu-

Guerrilla training of children by members of Fatah, the Palestine Liberation Front, and other Palestinian groups. The reason for these camps can be summed up by the words of one member: "Our struggle could last for generations."

dents founded the Arab Nationalists' Movement in the early 1950s. Their hope was to bind all Arabs, not just Palestinians, into a great national movement. Thrown out of Lebanon for their activities, Habash moved the ANM to Egypt, where it expanded into a broad-based organization of mostly professional people and intellectuals.

In 1964, partly as a response to Fatah, the Arab Nationalists' Movement set up a separate Palestinian group, the National Front for the Liberation of Palestine. This group in 1967 merged with two others to create the Popular Front for the Liberation of Palestine (PFLP). In its first public statement, the PFLP announced, "The only weapon left in the hands of the people is revolutionary violence."

The growth of such independent groups as Fatah and the PFLP faltered when a powerful rival organization appeared in Cairo.

NASSER FORMS THE PLO

Uneasy about the many shadowy Palestinian groups operating in the Middle East, Egypt's President Nasser in 1964 decided to form a Palestinian umbrella organization he could control. Nasser didn't want Palestinian terrorists to start a war with Israel, a war that Egypt would have to fight, and which he knew Egypt would lose to the better-organized and better-equipped Israelis.

Nasser called a summit meeting of Arab governments and convinced them to form a Palestine Liberation Organization. Technically, the PLO became the executive branch of the Palestinian National Council, a sort of parliament in exile. Some 422 Palestinian representatives, mostly conservatives picked by Arab governments, attended the May 1964 meeting founding the Palestine National Council. They elected Nasser's choice,

Ahmad Shuqairi, a Palestinian lawyer and diplomat, as first PLO president. Shuqairi picked the first executive committee of fifteen people. The committee set up a Palestine National Fund to raise and disburse money. Every Palestinian refugee was asked to contribute, as were Arab governments.

Khalad al-Hassan and several other Fatah representatives attended the conference as observers, but officially Fatah boycotted the first session of the National Council. The Fatah people said the PLO was too much under the thumb of Arab governments. Al-Hassan also charged that the Council was an undemocratic "elected dictatorship" controlled by Arab regimes.

Shuqairi wrote the PLO charter, or Covenant, which was adopted on June 1, 1964. The organization's purpose was the liberation of Palestine. The Covenant declared: "Palestine is an Arab homeland," and condemned Zionism as imperialist and racist. The Covenant specifically left out both the Gaza Strip and the West Bank from the area over which the PLO claimed jurisdiction—because Egypt controlled the first, and Jordan held the second. The PLO therefore claimed control over nothing more or less than Israel.

A few months later, the Arab League agreed at a meeting in Alexandria to form a Palestine Liberation Army as the military arm of the PLO. When it was finally set up, the army consisted of separate units of Palestinians in Arab states, commanded not by Palestinians, but by officers of the host governments.

Palestinians now had an organization and an army, but both were puppets of Arab states that had no desire to fight Israel over Palestine. In fact, Nasser tried to enforce a ban on Palestinian commando and terrorist activities, saying it was not yet the proper time for military action against Israel. Palestinian militants, including Fatah, felt they had been sold out. Both Fatah and the Popular Front for the Liberation of Palestine boycotted the PLO.

However, the PLO captured the fancy of ordinary people who thought they now had a strong voice to represent them, and an army to fight for them. Fatah lost 80 to 90 percent of its cells to the PLO and its new army. Funds dried up.

FATAH BEGINS COMMANDO RAIDS

Though its numbers shrank dramatically, Fatah did not disappear, partly because it had gained a new ally. A new revolutionary government in Syria let Fatah set up combat training camps there. They became, in effect, terrorist training camps. Arafat sold his construction business in Kuwait and moved to Syria.

As Fatah planned raids, most of its leaders took war names: Abu Ammar for Arafat, Abu Jihad for al-Wazir, Um Jihad for Intissar al-Wazir, Abu Iyad for Khalaf. Most of the time, Fatah's Central Committee was scattered, as individuals frequently and secretly shifted operations from Kuwait to Algeria, Lebanon, or Syria.

Arafat and Khalaf argued that Fatah should attack Israel immediately, and they went ahead with plans over the opposition of some other members of the Central Committee. Fatah's first raid, planned for New Year's Eve, 1965, and publicized by the group, never actually happened. Even after it was called off because word had been leaked, Arafat passed out public relations releases as if the raid had taken place. Another raid a few days later also failed. Both raids had been planned to damage a new Israeli canal diverting water from the upper Jordan River into Israel. The Arab states had threatened war over the water project, and Fatah's leaders knew they could attract great attention if they could damage the canal.

By 1966, Fatah commandos were entering Israel from bases in Jordan, the Gaza Strip, Syria, and Lebanon. They did not strike Israeli military installations; their targets were civilians. Their goals were to demoralize Israel's people and to publicize the Palestinian cause. When the first Fatah fedayeen died in a raid, Fatah made much of his death, calling him a martyr to the Palestinian cause.

Arafat had his first big falling out with the collective leadership of Fatah when he ran raids the group had not approved. Khalad al-Hassan argued fiercely that Arafat had to be reined in if Fatah was to remain a democratic organization with group leadership. The group suspended Arafat from the Fatah executive committee, but he remained in the field with fedayeen raiders. Al-Wazir became the military commander.

To run more raids, the group desperately needed weapons. It sent al-Wazir (Abu Jihad) to Europe to locate arms dealers willing to sell to Fatah. The trip was expected to take months, because al-Wazir would have to dodge Israeli security agents. The question arose of who could coordinate Fatah's military operations while al-Wazir was gone. Arafat was in suspension, and he wanted to be in the field anyway. No one else was available who knew all the key people. Al-Wazir suggested his wife Intissar (Um Jihad) as temporary chief of military operations for Fatah, saying she knew his methods and contacts and could be trusted. She was also prepared to die for the cause rather than submit to questioning. For six months, Intissar's apartment in Beirut became operations headquarters for Fatah's raiders.

Late in September 1965, while al-Wazir was still in Europe, Arafat learned that the Lebanese were moving to arrest dozens of Palestinians in Beirut. Fearing for Intissar, Arafat raced by taxi from Damascus to Beirut, then had the taxi wait while he burst into the al-Wazirs' apartment. He gave Intissar twenty minutes to gather documents and personal items, woke her two sons, and helped them dress and gather clothes for the journey. Then he hustled them all into the waiting cab for the trip back to Syria.

All of them faced arrest at any time. That same year Arafat was jailed in Lebanon. He and others were again arrested in Syria in 1966. In fact, the Syrians for a short time had all the key Fatah people in the same jail, but decided to release them.

Despite the arrests and despite loss of numbers to the rival PLO, Fatah had begun to grow again. Fatah raids into Israel put added pressure on the PLO and Arab governments to step up their own hostile actions against Israel. Such raids helped provoke the war of 1967 that catapulted Fatah and Arafat into new leadership roles, and lost new lands to Israel.

CHAPTER 4

"OUT OF THE ASHES OF THIS DISASTROUS WAR . . ."

In a refugee village north of the Dead Sea in Jordan, a vastly outnumbered Fatah force held off an armored Israeli assault for several hours, and Yasir Arafat became an Arab hero. Fatah lost the battle, and Israeli troops swept over the village of Karameh. Yet before they did, a tiny Palestinian force had stood its ground, forcing Israeli tanks to retreat briefly. It was a victory of sorts, a victory Arabs needed badly in 1968.

When the fight took place, the Arab world was reeling in shock and humiliation after losing a swift, disastrous war to Israel. Karameh offered a glimmer of pride. By chance, the word Karameh means "honor" or "dignity" in Arabic, and the battle of Karameh wrapped Arafat and Fatah in honors. After Karameh, Arafat emerged as the leader not only of Fatah, but of a reorganized PLO. Only months before, he had been suspended from Fatah's ruling committee because of unauthorized raids. The Six Day War and Karameh changed all that. The war intensified Arab nationalism, and brought Arafat's generation into the forefront of Palestinian affairs.

THE SIX DAY WAR

In May 1967, Israel's political and military leaders knew that the Arabs were massing to annihilate Israel. President Nasser of Egypt had ordered UN peace-keeping troops out of the Sinai, moved Egyptian troops into positions along the Israeli border, closed the Suez Canal, and blocked Israel's outlet to the sea. "Our basic objective," Nasser said on May 26, "will be to destroy Israel." Iraq, Syria, and Jordan also moved forces into combat-ready stations.

Israel decided to strike first. On June 5, 1967, waves of Israeli planes destroyed most of the Egyptian, Syrian, Iraqi, and Jordanian air forces. Massed Israeli armor and infantry rolled across the Sinai desert toward Suez. In fewer than six days, Israeli forces crushed the combined armies of Egypt, Syria, Iraq, and Jordan. For the second time, Israelis captured the Sinai from Egypt. They also took the strategic Golan Heights overlooking Galilee from Syria, and drove Jordanian troops from the West Bank. The Arab states had vowed to drive the Israelis into the sea; instead the Arabs had suffered a devastating defeat. Israeli leaders had pleaded with King Hussein of Jordan to stay out of the war. By sending in his forces and then losing, the king had lost a large chunk of his country to Israel.

When the war ended, Israel occupied a land area four times the size of Israel before the war. The Six Day War created more Palestinian refugees as some 200,000 Arabs fled to the East Bank in Jordan from the newly occupied territories. The war also left a million and a half Arabs in lands occupied by Israel.

During the fighting, Israel captured the half of Jerusalem that had remained in Arab hands, and vowed never to yield it. Israelis bulldozed the walls that had divided Jerusalem, annexed East Jerusalem as part of the state of Israel, and made the city the new capital of Israel.

The Israelis did not officially annex the West Bank or the Gaza Strip, and in fact offered to return most of the captured territory if Arab nations would make peace by acknowledging Israel's right to exist. The deal offered was land for peace. Once again Arab leaders failed to compromise or accept reality. At an Arab summit conference in August 1967, the Arab countries announced a formula of "three no's"—no peace, no negotiations, and no recognition of Israel. The Arab states vowed to fight again.

Once again Palestinians were the biggest losers as the Arab governments postured. Palestinians in the West Bank and Gaza were left in limbo. They soon found themselves under Israeli military government. Despite Arab boasts to fight again, the Six Day War exposed the total military superiority of Israeli forces over the combined Arab states. The war not only defeated the Arabs, it humiliated them.

FATAH REBOUNDS

The day the war started, Fatah's military commander, Abu Jihad (al-Wazir), was in Germany buying arms. He flew home, met Arafat at the Yarmuk refugee camp, and the two set off for the Golan Heights in Arafat's Volkswagen. As they joined Fatah fedayeen attacking Israeli positions from the Golan Heights, they passed Syrian troops in retreat. The war was already all but over.

Within days after the cease-fire ending the war, Fatah's Central Committee met in Damascus to decide whether to give up or start over. Abu Jihad recalled that he and others could not discuss what had happened without weeping. Some said they might as well scatter and build new lives somewhere in the Arab world.

Almost alone, Arafat refused to accept that their defeat was permanent. He argued doggedly that Israeli occupation of Gaza and the West Bank would unite Palestinians as nothing had before. Arafat said that instead of giving up, it was time for Fatah to shift from Phase A in standard guerrilla planning (terrorist nuisance raids) to Phase B, setting up operation centers in the occupied territories and infiltrating enemy positions.

Khalad al-Hassan, who had insisted a year earlier on suspending Arafat from the Central Committee because he was staging raids on his own, still feared that Arafat might turn into a dictator if put back in a position of power. Al-Hassan balked at Arafat's suggestion that Fatah start terrorist raids immediately. Arafat left the early meetings discouraged, sure he had lost.

Then al-Hassan's brother Hani arrived from Germany with startling news. Hundreds of Palestinian students had left schools in Europe when the Six Day War began. A group of 450 of them were training in Algeria and would shortly arrive in the occupied territories. If Arafat was ready to resume the fight, Hani al-Hassan and the students were behind him.

Within two weeks, the committee swung behind Arafat, and named him Fatah's official spokesman. On June 23 Arafat announced that Fatah was shifting operations into the occupied territories, and that raids on Israel would start soon. Because the Arab world was desperate for face-saving news, Beirut papers played up Fatah's grandiose promises. They quoted Arafat's pledge: "Out of this disastrous war will arise the phoenix of a free Arab Palestine."[1]

Fatah leaders visited refugee camps, urging people to become fedayeen, to train for terrorist raids into Israel. They handed out pamphlets on how to make gasoline bombs; they urged boycotts of Israeli businesses. Arafat and other Fatah recruiters had little luck among the demoralized refugees, but student commandos began to arrive from training camps in Algeria and China. An Arab summit conference in 1967 had promised funds from Arab states for fedayeen groups, and Fatah was able to get arms and money from several Arab governments.

Meanwhile, Israeli agents combed the occupied territories, jailing suspected terrorists. They blew up the homes of known Fatah families. In less than three months, the Israelis captured more than a thousand Fatah fighters. Nearly 90 percent of Hani al-Hassan's student fedayeen were either killed or captured.

Though the West Bank and Gaza swarmed with informers and double agents, Arafat eluded capture. A master of disguise, he seemed to have a sixth sense for danger. Once he slipped through an Israeli dragnet dressed as a woman and carrying a baby. He was disguised as a shepherd when Israeli agents searched a bus, but ignored the "shepherd." Another time he was about to enter a Fatah "safe house" in East Jerusalem disguised as an old man, when he paused outside. He sensed danger and left, less than half an hour before Israeli soldiers surrounded the house.

KARAMEH

In 1968, a strong pocket of resistance to Israeli occupation of the West Bank had developed in the village of Karameh on the Jordan side of the river. Villagers were so embittered by the death and destruction caused by Israeli shelling that they invited Fatah fedayeen to move in. From their base at Karameh, Fatah terrorists launched a series of raids, planting land mines and other explosives in Israel, almost always against civilian targets. On March 18, an Israeli school bus struck a Fatah bomb, killing one person and injuring twenty-eight. Israel readied a major attack on Karameh in response.

Exactly what happened next is one of those incidents in Arafat's life where eyewitness accounts do not agree. According to the official story, Arafat was in Karameh the night before the Israelis attacked on March 21. He rallied defenders in a stirring speech to stand up and fight. Other accounts say that he slipped out before the real fighting (as Abu Jihad definitely did), and left the defense to Salah Tamari, a twenty-three-year-old Bedouin from Bethlehem who had been in Fatah for five years. By these accounts, it was Tamari who ignored advice to evacuate, and who rallied Karameh's defenders.

All accounts agree that the people of Karameh were warned by Israeli pamphlets, Jordanian officers, and Israeli loudspeaker trucks that an attack was planned, and that civilians should flee. Fatah's commander was reminded that the first rule of guerrilla warfare is to slip away when faced by superior force, in order to survive to fight another day. Whether it was Arafat or Tamari, some Fatah commander made a moving speech urging that Karameh was the time and place to take a stand, although they could not hope to win.

A defending force of fewer than 300 hid in tunnels and inside buildings as Israeli helicopters, tanks, and rocket launchers, plus a column of at least 1,500 troops crossed the river before dawn. The hopelessly outnumbered Karameh defenders held out all morning, but at a cost of 150-200 dead. Boys strapped dynamite to their bodies, then threw themselves under the tanks, blowing up both the Israeli armor and themselves. The Israelis withdrew briefly.

Despite such bravery, the Palestinians would have

been crushed sooner if Jordanian artillery in surrounding hills had not also pounded the Israeli column. By some accounts, Tamari had won this Jordanian support by appealing to the honor of fellow Bedouins among the Jordanian officers. Jordanian artillery covered the retreat of Fatah survivors. Sometime before the Israelis overran the village, Arafat escaped on a motorcycle to the village of Salt. Tamari also escaped, and he became Arafat's second in command on the West Bank.

Whether Arafat was actually in Karameh directing the fight or not, Fatah held off the armed might of Israel for a few hours despite overwhelming odds. The Arabs badly needed heroes, and Arafat became one overnight. Arab newspapers and television sang the praises of the heroes of Karameh. Arab folk singers composed songs about the "Heroes of the Return [to Palestine]." Foreign television teams filmed Fatah training camps, focusing on the young boys training to follow in the steps of the heroes of Karameh. In the two days after the battle, some 5,000 people, including some women, showed up in Salt to join Fatah.

FATAH TAKES OVER A REVISED PLO

Suddenly famous, Arafat and other Fatah leaders arranged to meet with Egypt's president Nasser. The Egyptian president not only agreed to provide them with arms, he also took Arafat under his political wing. When Nasser went to Moscow in 1968, he invited Arafat along and introduced him to the Soviet leaders. The Egyptian president wanted Arafat to hear personally from the Soviets that the USSR would not support Arabs in a war against Israel. Alan Hart calls the Soviet trip the "end stop on a journey into reality" for Arafat.[2]

Nasser also encouraged Arafat to merge Fatah with

the weak and divided Palestine Liberation Organization. Nasser urged Arafat to have Fatah loyalists join the PLO, knowing that the well-organized Fatah would soon dominate the PLO.

Meanwhile, at Nasser's prodding, the Palestine National Council (PNC) met in July 1968 to revise the PLO. No longer would the council's membership consist of individuals and traditional leaders. Instead, the PNC, as the legislative arm of the PLO, was to be made up of delegates of Palestinian groups, including fedayeen, students, and worker organizations. Of 105 seats in the reorganized PNC, 57 went to fedayeen groups including 33 assigned to Fatah. Most of the student and worker groups were also tied to Fatah. For all practical purposes, Fatah captured the PLO.

The Palestine National Council also rewrote the Palestine National Covenant, bringing it in line with Fatah's thinking. The new document dedicated the PLO to the elimination of the state of Israel through armed struggle. (See the Appendix for extracts from the charter.)

With new rules and new delegates, the fifth PNC met in February 1969. The council chose an executive committee with four Fatah members, including Khalad al-Hassan and Farouq Qaddumi. With Nasser looking on, the executive committee picked Arafat as chairman of the PLO. Arafat wept with pleasure. At the same session, the PNC adopted Fatah's position that "the objective of the Palestinian people is to establish a democratic society in Palestine open to all Palestinians—Muslims, Christians, and Jews."[3]

In 1969, Egypt's President Gamal Abdel Nasser shares a drink with Arafat, as Arab leaders arrive in Morocco to discuss plans for war against Israel.

Arafat immediately began trying to draw other fedayeen groups into the PLO, a decision that has led to endless quarreling and rifts in the organization. Within a year, all major guerrilla or terrorist groups had enrolled under the PLO umbrella. Each group, however, was free to continue its own separate existence, and to take stands totally at odds with one another.

This structure made the PLO an unwieldly organization in which any radical group could undercut the stands taken by the official leadership. Avner Yaniv, an Israeli professor of international relations, has written that Arafat's nominal leadership of the PLO masked the fact that he could run the organization only by consensus. "In effect, the PLO was in 1967–70—and has remained to date—a loose, voluntary confederation in which the militants (who are often in the service of one or another Arab government) basically call the shots."[4] He notes that if Habash or others disagreed with Arafat, and if he tried to discipline them, the PLO would break apart and Arafat's claim of being spokesman for the Palestinian cause would suffer. (In 1990, after the Iraqi invasion of Kuwait, just such a splintering seemed possible.)

Within the reorganized PLO, Fatah, as the largest and best-organized group, pictured itself in the late 1960s as an Arab nationalist organization with a single goal— the liberation of Palestine from Israeli control. Fatah made no commitment to any political "ism." Its message was simple, tough nationalism. Fatah offered no outline of what kind of government would operate a future Palestinian state. That would be decided after Palestinians retook their homeland, said Fatah's founders.

By contrast, some fedayeen groups in the PLO were committed not only to liberation but also to revolution to topple existing Arab governments. Habash's Popular Front for the Liberation of Palestine was (and still is) a militant Marxist group. Formed in the 1967 merger of

A group of women fedayeen receive rifle instruction.

three smaller groups, the PFLP worked to stir up communist revolutions in the Arab world, particularly in Jordan, which it considered part of Palestine. Habash became Arafat's main rival for leadership of the PLO, and Arafat's sharpest critic on the left.

Habash and other Marxist radicals accused Fatah of being too middle class, partly because Fatah said it did not meddle in the internal affairs of Arab states. The radicals plotted social revolution and sent terrorists around the world to make their point. Rivals also criticized Fatah for drawing support from conservative Arab governments.

SUPPORT FROM THE
SAUDI KING

Unlike some guerrilla groups, Fatah paid a regular wage to its fighters, and gave pensions to widows and children. In the crowded refugee camps, the PLO began to set up courts, run classes, and provide medical services. By 1968, some 1.7 million Palestinian refugees lived in the camps, and the PLO tried to offer them some of the services of a government.

To buy weapons, pay salaries, and fund operations in the refugee camps, Fatah's central committee prowled Arab capitals, seeking money from the oil-rich states. Khalad al-Hassan pulled off the big coup by winning the ear of King Faisal of Saudi Arabia. After waiting for weeks in the Saudi capital, al-Hassan finally got an appointment with the king, one of the most conservative rulers in the Middle East. Al-Hassan told Faisal that the PLO did not want to rely only on the support it had been getting from China, Algeria, and other revolutionary governments. He stressed Fatah's policy of staying out of the affairs of Arab countries, and said the PLO's only goal was to liberate Palestine. Faisal agreed to help with

Arafat with King Faisal of Saudi Arabia

both money and arms. He also agreed to al-Hassan's suggestion to levy a tax on Palestinians who worked in Saudi Arabia to support the PLO. Two weeks later, twenty-eight Saudi army trucks delivered arms and ammunition, enough to supply many PLO bases. In the next two decades, Saudi Arabia was a major source of funds for the PLO. The PLO tax on Palestinians was instituted in many other Arab nations and became an important source of PLO income.

TROUBLE FROM JORDAN

Using the Saudi arms and money, PLO terrorists began raiding Israel from bases in Jordan. King Hussein knew that letting the fedayeen operate from Jordan was risky, because Israel might attack Jordan in response. However, for a while well-armed Palestinians seemed too powerful for him to challenge openly. The king also knew that many Palestinians considered Jordan part of Palestine, and plotted to overthrow him to set up a Palestinian state. Leftists and radicals in the PLO used the slogan, "The road to Tel Aviv [Israel's capital] leads through Amman [Jordan's capital]." In other words, first overthrow Jordan, then Israel. For three years, the king watched helplessly as fedayeen chipped away at his authority.

Fedayeen groups, including branches of the PLO, grew so strong that they became almost a state within a state in Jordan. They ran their own radio station, courts, and police force. They flaunted their power with mass demonstrations and strikes. Along the Israeli border, fedayeen ousted local people from some villages, turning the villages into armed camps. By 1970, Habash's PFLP and other left-wing groups had become reckless in their challenges to Hussein's authority. They provoked armed clashes and mass demonstrations mocking the king. They set up roadblocks and hijacked Jordanian trucks. They even offended devout Muslims by broadcasting communist propaganda from the towers of mosques.

Although urged to use armed force to control the PFLP and other extremists, Arafat refused. According to Khalad al-Hassan, Arafat tried to be a voice for calm. "At all our meetings he spoke only of the need for reconciliation with Hussein's regime."[5] Ignoring such advice, PFLP assassins twice in 1970 tried to murder the king. The second attempt was on September 1. Five days later, the PFLP hijacked four international airlines, and forced two of them down at a Jordanian airfield.

Hussein felt they had finally gone too far. On September 17, the king loosed his Bedouin troops on the Palestinians. Jordanian troops rampaged through refugee camps as they overran fedayeen bases. Fires burned out of control. Ambulances were stopped and the wounded taken out and butchered. At least 5,000 Palestinians died; thousands more were wounded. The rampage left a smoldering legacy of hate among many Palestinians against the Jordanian ruler and his army.

Nasser persuaded King Hussein to sign a cease-fire with Arafat on September 27. In the agreement, the king agreed to allow PLO fighters to live in Jordan's cities. However, Nasser died the next day of a heart attack. Arafat and other PLO chiefs were devastated by this death but worse was to follow. After Nasser's death, Hussein scrapped the agreement, and ordered his troops to drive the PLO from Jordan.

Many of the survivors fled to Syria; some waded across the Jordan River into Israel. Others joined the Palestinians already living in Lebanon. Jordanians caught Khalaf and jailed him, but Arafat escaped wearing robes loaned to him by a Kuwaiti prince.

After the PLO was expelled from Jordan, fedayeen commando groups accused the Arab states of betraying them once again by failing to come to their aid. Fatah also accused Habash and the PFLP of being extremists and of bringing down Jordan's fury on them all. Yet in the wake of the Jordanian massacres, Fatah's leaders also vowed revenge, and despite the reservations of Arafat and others, formed a secret terrorist group to overthrow King Hussein. The new organization, Black September, violated one of Fatah's own rules—staying out of the politics of other countries. It also signaled a new, more violent phase for both Fatah and the PLO.

On November 22, 1967, the Security Council of the United Nations approved a resolution outlining the basis for peace between the State of Israel and the Arab countries. In a formal agreement signed in 1978 at Camp David, the United States, Israel, and Egypt endorsed Resolution 242 "in all its parts." The Resolution states:

The Security Council,

Expressing its continued concern with the grave situation in the Middle East,

Emphasizing the inadmissibility of the acquisition of territory by war and the need to work for a just and lasting peace in which every state in the area can live in security,

Emphasizing further that all Member States in their acceptance of the Charter of the United Nations have undertaken a commitment to act in accordance with Article 2 of the Charter

1. *Affirms* that the fulfilment of Charter principles requires the establishment of a just and lasting peace in the Middle East which should include the application of both the following principles:

(i) Withdrawal of Israel armed forces from territories occupied in the recent conflict;

(ii) Termination of all claims or states of belligerency and respect for the acknowledgment of the sovereignty, territorial integrity and political independence of every State in the area and their right to live in peace within secure and recognized boundaries free from threats or acts of force.

2. *Affirms further* the necessity

(a) For guaranteeing freedom of navigation through international waterways in the area;

(b) For achieving a just settlement of the refugee problem;

(c) For guaranteeing the territorial inviolability and political independence of every State in the area, through measures including the establishment of demilitarized zones:

3. *Requests* the Secretary-General to designate a Special Representative to proceed to the Middle East to establish and maintain contacts with the States concerned in order to promote agreement and assist efforts to achieve a peaceful and accepted settlement in accordance with the provisions and principles in this resolution;

4. *Requests* the Secretary-General to report to the Security Council on the progress of the efforts of the Special Representative as soon as possible.

CHAPTER 5

THE USE OF TERROR

In the hours before dawn, wearing ski masks to hide their faces, eight Black September terrorists slipped into a dormitory and kidnapped eleven Israeli athletes at the 1972 Olympics at Munich, West Germany. The terrorists killed two athletes who resisted them, then tossed a note out a window stating their demands: the release of 200 Palestinian prisoners in Israeli jails, and a jet to fly the terrorists to an Arab country.

Israel has a firm policy of not dealing with terrorists, and the government asked the Germans not to yield to the demands. After hours of negotiations, German police told the terrorists they would take them and the hostages by helicopters to an airport, where a jet would be waiting to fly them to Egypt. At the airport, one Black Septembrist left each helicopter to check the plane. Before they could return to the helicopters, hidden German marksmen began firing. During the shoot-out that followed, the terrorists shot the nine athletes and blew up a helicopter with their bodies in it.

The Germans jailed the three surviving terrorists.

*Demonstrators march outside the Olympic
Village, calling for a halt to the 1972
games, as armed Arab terrorists held
a dozen Israeli team members hostage.*

*A jet dissolves into debris and smoke as Arab
guerrillas who hijacked the plane in 1970
touch off the explosives they had placed in
it earlier. The terrorists took the passengers
off the plane before destroying it.*

However, within weeks, they were released in exchange for eleven hostages taken when Palestinians hijacked a German Lufthansa airplane.

The attack on the Munich Olympics and the Lufthansa hijacking were part of an epidemic of hijacking, kidnapping, bombing, and terrorist murder that peaked in the 1970s, but continues into the 1990s. In the eyes of much of the world, "Palestinian" and "terrorist" have become almost synonymous.

Palestinian terrorism has taken two main forms. First are raids and infiltrations into Israel in which terrorists plant bombs and explosives in movie theaters, restaurants, buses, and other public places. The targets of this form of terrorism are civilians in Israel and in the occupied territories. The second form of terrorism reaches beyond the Middle East, and involves hijacking, hostage-taking, murder, and other headline-catching acts around the world. Though some of the international victims are Israelis, many others are people who simply happen to be in a place picked as a terrorist target.

Hijacking began in 1968, when Habash's PFLP commandeered an Israeli aircraft and flew it to Algeria. Afterward, Israel tightened its air security, making it all but impossible to hijack an Israeli plane. Terrorists then began seizing the planes of countries allied with Israel. In September 1970, the PFLP managed to hijack four planes—two American, one Swiss, and one British. The terrorists flew two of the jets to a desert airstrip in Jordan, and after releasing most of the hostages, blew up the planes. The remaining hostages were released later in exchange for PFLP prisoners being held in European jails. The choice of Jordan as a landing spot was meant to embarrass King Hussein. However, the plan boomeranged because it gave Hussein the excuse he wanted to send his army to smash the PLO in Jordan.

BLACK SEPTEMBER

Fatah formed a terrorist army and named it in reaction to Jordan's destruction of PLO forces in September 1970. In setting up Black September to run terror operations against civilians around the globe, Fatah shifted tactics away from its stated policies of striking only in Israel and in areas controlled by Israeli armed forces, and of not interfering in the affairs of other nations.

The three top leaders of Black September were close associates of Salah Khalaf (Abu Iyad). He claimed that Black September emerged spontaneously among angry fedayeen from several commando groups as a reaction to the death and humiliation caused when Jordanian troops killed thousands of Palestinians and drove the PLO from Jordan. Israeli intelligence sources say that Abu Iyad masterminded the group, that Black September was a front behind which Fatah could carry out murderous activities. According to the Israelis, the other top Black September insiders were Mohammed Daoud Awda (Abu Daoud) and Ali Hassan Salameh. Arrested and tortured in Jordan after a failed attempt to kidnap Jordanian leaders in 1973, Abu Daoud broadcast a confession that there was no such thing as Black September; it was a cover to protect Fatah.[1]

Black September's first terror strike murdered Jordan's prime minister, Wasfi Tal, in November 1971. The following year, the group hijacked a Sabena jet and seized the Israeli embassy in Bangkok, Thailand. In 1973, Black Septembrists invaded a reception at the Saudi Arabian embassy in Khartoum, Sudan, and took several diplomats hostage. The terrorists issued a long list of demands: release by Jordan of Abu Daoud and his group and of Jordanian officers held for plotting against King Hussein; release by the United States of Sirhan Sirhan, the man who killed President John F. Kennedy's brother,

Robert Kennedy; the release of several German terrorists; and the release of several female Arab terrorists held by Israel. When the demands were rejected, the Black Septembrists machine-gunned two Americans and a Belgian hostage.

These so-called external operations were staged to boost Fatah's faltering status among Palestinians. Arafat and Fatah faced strong challenges to their dominance in the PLO after the Jordan fiasco. Breakaway fedayeen groups were running their own terrorist raids, skyjackings, and murders, and in the process were gaining recruits.

Fatah's leaders apparently decided that even though acts of international terrorism did not advance their cause, they might lose control of the PLO if they did not prove themselves willing to use such tactics as well. Khalad al-Hassan, one of Fatah's more moderate insiders, insists that Fatah's leaders had to link themselves with terrorists in order to gain credibility among the rank and file. Only then, he claims, could they take control and "turn off the terror tap." Fatah spokesmen claim that Abu Iyad planned the Munich operation as a flamboyant gesture to gain world attention for the Palestinian cause.

Whatever the truth of such claims, Black September drew recruits not only from Fatah but from other fedayeen groups. According to Albert Parry, an authority on terrorism, Black September began with 150 carefully chosen people, and grew to about 300 to mid-1974. He says it had a special treasury, separate from Fatah's other funds, of some $150 million in 1972.[2]

Sometime after Munich (exactly how soon is disputed), the Fatah Central Committee withdrew its backing for Black September, and sent orders for Fatah people not to participate in Black September raids. By late 1974, Black September officially had ceased to function as an offshoot of Fatah.

However, two well-known Fatah members closely linked with Black September ignored the orders and continued to spread terror. One was Abu Mahmoud, Black September's link with Libya's revolutionary government. The other was Sabri al-Banna, better known as Abu Nidal, one of the world's most ruthless terrorists. Several of the most horrifying terrorist actions in the past twenty-five years were planned by Abu Nidal. He broke with the PLO in 1973, and formed his own terrorist group in Iraq. Abu Nidal called his group the Fatah Revolutionary Council; it had no connection with Fatah, though, and is not part of the PLO. The PLO's Fatah, in fact, voted a death sentence against Abu Nidal, but has not been able to carry it out. Abu Nidal has murdered several PLO leaders whom he considered too moderate.

Most observers think Arafat tried to curb international terrorism after 1973 not because he felt any distaste for murder or kidnapping, but on practical grounds. International terrorism did nothing to get Palestine back, and turned world opinion against Palestinians in general. However, Arafat continued to direct raids into Israel, to shell Israeli settlements, and to conduct other activities that most civilized people consider terrorism because the targets are civilians rather than government or military establishments.

JUSTIFYING VIOLENCE

To most Palestinians, an attack on Israel that kills civilians is not terrorism. Palestinians insist that Israelis took their homeland and installed an army to defend their gains. Therefore, Palestinians fight in the only way left to them. What an Israeli or American calls terrorism, Palestinians view as a legitimate tactic in an armed struggle to regain Palestine. Violence, they claim, is the only weapon left to an oppressed people.

Even the words used are loaded with emotion and bias. Palestinians call those who raid and bomb Israeli settlements commandos, partisans, resistance fighters, freedom fighters, guerrillas, or fedayeen (people willing to die for a cause). To Israelis and most Americans the same people are murderers, terrorists, saboteurs, criminal thugs. When Israeli air strikes kill Palestinian civilians, including children, Palestinians demand to know why such raids are not called terrorist attacks.

Interviewing Palestinian refugees in Lebanon in the 1970s, British journalist Jonathan Dimbleby met an old man who said he wished he could have been in on an operation like the one in Munich. The Black September men are "heroes to our people," this man said. After hearing many such comments, Dimbleby concluded that Palestinians in the refugee camps felt so trapped and degraded that they built up a violent, wild resolve to fight Israel. "It is the wildfire passion of such individuals, stoked up by the revolution, that it is now the awesome task of the PLO to direct and contain,"[3] Dimbleby said in his 1979 book, *The Palestinians*.

David Shipler, an American journalist who covered the Middle East for the *New York Times* from 1979 to 1984, described similar attitudes several years later. In his Pulitzer Prize-winning book, *Arab and Jew: Wounded Spirits in a Promised Land,* Shipler said Palestinians feel dehumanized because they were driven from their land and live as stateless people in exile or in refugee camps. Shipler quotes a Jerusalem Arab who says that when someone has lost so much, he can afford to be wild. In such a climate, terrorists are considered heroes.

Shipler points out too that violence and lawlessness have long been common in the Middle East. Among Palestinians, violence has become an accepted part of the culture. A Palestinian terrorist is therefore not an outsider to society, but someone viewed as acting in society's behalf. Most Palestinians tend to see nothing wrong with PLO attacks on Israeli civilians, even on children. When a 1974 raid killed twenty-one students, Palestinians reacted angrily to criticism that Palestinians were killing innocent children. According to them, Israelis had killed and maimed Palestinian children by bombing refugee camps.

Islam teaches that a person who dies in a *jihad,* or holy war, becomes a martyr and goes directly to paradise. Early in Fatah's development, Arafat adopted the idea of martyrs, fighters who die for a cause. Pictures of Fatah fedayeen killed in action were posted prominently in refugee camps. New Fatah members took the names of "martyrs" who died in the "sacred war" against Israel.

Such justifications for terror became part of the curriculum—along with bomb-making, sabotage, and other skills—at terrorist training camps not only in the Middle East but also in countries around the world run by radical governments. Palestinian commandos in the 1970s could go for training to China, North Korea, Vietnam, Bulgaria, or to Lebanon to enroll in the PLO's own training centers. Israeli sources claim that in just eighteen months in 1980–81, PLO and other fedayeen groups brought 2,250 terrorists from twenty-nine countries to the Middle East for training.[4] In the process, close ties developed between terrorists of many countries, forming an international network. The Black September terrorists who captured the Olympic athletes, for instance, got help from Bulgarian communists.

ESCALATING TERROR

Each terrorist attack on Israelis invited massive counterstrike. Israelis, for more than forty years the target of relentless hit-and-run tactics, tend to view all PLO attacks as the actions of terrorist murderers. After the World

War II massacre of millions of Jews in Nazi Germany, Israelis swore that Jews would never again be helpless victims; the Israeli government will protect its people wherever, whenever, however.

After the Munich massacre, Israeli jets pounded Palestinian refugee camps, killing fourteen civilians, while ground troops invaded refugee camps in Lebanon and killed many more. After a 1968 attack on an Israeli jet at the Athens airport, Israeli commandos slipped into the Beirut airport and blew up thirteen Arab-owned planes.

After a formal debate by the government in 1972, Israel's Mossad (security agency) began tracking down and killing known Palestinian terrorists and PLO leaders. Mossad agents mailed package bombs to PLO offices and planted bombs in PLO cars. Disguised as fedayeen, a Mossad squad burst into two PLO apartments in Beirut in April 1973, showering those inside with a hail of bullets. Abu Iyad, who had been staying in one of the apartments, happened to be away. The Mossad commandos not only killed three Black Septembrists, they also made off with three filing cabinets of Black September records.[5]

Though Arafat and Fatah may have dropped out of the international kidnapping and hijacking business, other Palestinian groups did not. In 1975 Habash decided to disband the PFLP international terror unit, but a splinter group linked with the Soviet Union, the Popular Democratic Front for the Liberation of Palestine (PDFLP), continued its international attacks. Though these groups were often identified simply as Palestinian terrorists, they were not directly under Arafat's control, and in fact opposed him within the PLO.

The following accounts are only some of the most spectacular acts of terrorism by non-Fatah groups in the 1970s and 1980s.

Habash's PFLP recruited three Japanese terrorists for a suicide hijacking of an Air France flight to Israel in May 1972. After landing at Israel's Lod airport, the hijackers opened fire with submachine guns, killing twenty-five people and wounding seventy-eight. Most of the dead were Christian pilgrims coming to the Holy Land from Puerto Rico. Two of the terrorists committed suicide, but the third was captured before he could do so.

Israel's most spectacular rescue of people hijacked by terrorists took place in 1976, at the airport in Entebbe, Uganda. A splinter group of the PFLP hijacked an Air France plane and forced the pilot to land at Entebbe. About a hundred passengers were released, but ninety Jewish passengers were kept on the plane. Israel flew in a specially trained anti-hijacking team, and rescued all but three passengers.

Soviet-backed terrorists in May 1974 seized an Israeli school in the Galilee village of Maalot. The terrorists held a hundred teenagers and five teachers hostage for sixteen hours while they wired explosives to the walls. When Israeli forces stormed the school, the Palestinians shot and killed twenty-two people and wounded fifty-six others. In retaliation, Israeli planes bombed PLO strongholds in Lebanon, killing fifty people and injuring two hundred.

Younger children died in 1980, when terrorists captured a "children's house" at an Israeli kibbutz (collective settlement) at Misgav Am. In Israeli collective settlements, children live in houses apart from their parents. Five terrorists carrying Russian rifles and a grenade launcher managed to slip through a mine field shortly after midnight. They cut several fences undetected to enter a concrete house where four children slept. The guerrillas grabbed two of the children, shot the adult with them, and then ran to barricade themselves in another house where four toddlers, aged two and three, slept in cribs. Before the shooting was over, one child had died, five were wounded, and all five terrorists had been killed.

Israelis keep meticulous records of all attacks. They point out that though Fatah stopped staging international raids, Arafat's group ran many hit-and-run attacks in Israel and the occupied territories. Almost every attack was against unarmed civilians. According to Israeli sources, Arafat's second in command, Abu Jihad (al-Wazir), directed a Fatah attack in which saboteurs landed by boat from Lebanon, entered the Savoy Hotel in Tel Aviv, and killed eleven Israelis. Abu Jihad is also thought to have planned a 1978 attack on a bus near Tel Aviv in which thirty-three Israelis died.

Four Palestinians machine-gunned worshippers at a synagogue in Hebron in 1980, killing six and wounding sixteen. Two PLO groups claimed credit in 1983 for the bombing of an Israeli bus that killed six and wounded forty-one.

Each new instance of terrorist violence triggered an Israeli counterattack. Israelis deliberately hit back in force, taking more Palestinian lives in each counterstrike than were lost in the earlier attack on Israelis. An assassination team that was almost certainly from Israel's Mossad murdered Abu Jihad and his bodyguards in 1988 at his home in Tunis.

It is not possible in a book about Arafat and the PLO to detail the long list of terrorist acts by Palestinians such as Abu Nidal, who work outside the PLO umbrella. However, every hijacking, kidnapping, or other act of terrorism by Palestinians hardened Israeli determination not to negotiate with any part of the PLO, and blackened the PLO in the eyes of the world.

Shipler notes in his book that Arabs who oppose terrorism usually do so very, very quietly, and only among family and friends. Terrorism, he says, has evolved into

Terrorist attacks on Israel lead to Israeli attacks on Arabs. Reprisal raids are common, as the Israelis hope to hit guerrilla bases.

a routine part of Palestinian society.[6] It is accepted as a tool of combat and is not condemned by the society in which the PLO operates. This casual acceptance of actions condemned by most civilized societies is one reason Israelis are so wary of the PLO and any promises Arafat might make.

Arafat has been unable to curb international violence, and has generally been unwilling to end terrorism against Israeli civilians. While Fatah abandoned international terrorism, it had no such prohibition against terrorist raids within Israel. These attacks grew in intensity after 1977, when a new Israeli government under Menachem Begin encouraged Israelis to move to the West Bank as permanent settlers. Though Israel did not formally annex the West Bank and Gaza, Begin signalled his eagerness to do so. As more Israelis moved into permanent settlements, it seemed to Palestinians like a replay of 1948, when they first lost lands to Israel. The PLO has been relentless in its attacks on Israeli settlements in the West Bank, attacks the Israelis call terror and Palestinians call defense of a homeland.

By the early 1980s, vigilante groups among Israeli settlers in the West Bank and Gaza began revenge attacks on Palestinians. Thirty days after the end of the traditional Jewish mourning period for those killed at the Hebron synagogue, Israeli vigilantes planted bombs that maimed the Palestinian mayors of two West Bank communities. The difference between such Israeli acts of violence and Palestinian terrorism, say the Israelis, is that the Israeli government puts Jewish terrorists on trial and punishes them under a code of laws, while Palestinians hail the killers of innocent people as heroes.

As more Jewish settlers moved to the West Bank, Arafat struggled to build a new base in Lebanon, and to keep control of the badly split PLO.

CHAPTER 6

OLIVE BRANCH OR GUN?
(1971–82)

On November 13, 1974, wearing battle fatigues, a kaffiyeh head scarf, and a holster, Yasir Arafat stood before the United Nations General Assembly to open a debate on Palestine. The president of Lebanon introduced Arafat to the General Assembly. There was irony in that, for Lebanon was dissolving into a ruinous civil war in which the PLO was an unsettling force.

At the UN, Arafat spoke of the PLO dream of forming a democratic state in Palestine in place of a Jewish state. "When we speak of our common hopes for the Palestine of tomorrow, we include in our perspective all Jews now living in Palestine who choose to live with us there in peace and without discrimination."[1] In answer to charges that the PLO fosters terrorists, Arafat declared that no one is a terrorist who stands for a just cause.

"I have come bearing an olive branch [the symbol of peace] and a freedom fighter's gun. Do not let the olive branch fall from my hand." Actually, his holster was empty; the UN would not let him wear a gun. On

*Yasir Arafat addressing the 29th General
Assembly of the United Nations. No one is in
the Israeli section (left); Israel
boycotted the session at which Arafat spoke.*

this flamboyant note, though, he ended a speech heard by Palestinians over television and radio. Schools closed in the refugee camps to let students listen as Arafat addressed the world audience. Celebrations erupted in the camps at the end of the speech.

There was more to celebrate a week later when the General Assembly voted UN Resolution 3236, recognizing the rights of the Palestinian people to "self-determination, national independence and sovereignty." The UN also granted the PLO observer status, allowing a representative to sit in, but not to vote.

In 1974, the PLO seemed to be winning its quest for recognition and respectability; it was treated by many countries as the legitimate voice of a people with a legitimate claim and a legitimate grievance. Only two weeks before the UN speech, the Arab league had met in Rabat and declared the Palestinian Liberation Organization the "sole legitimate representative of the Palestinian people." Yet though they paid the organization lip service, conservative Arab regimes remained wary of the PLO, viewing it as a school for revolutionaries. It was no secret that since 1972 the Soviet Union had been a major arms supplier to the PLO, or that the PLO had close ties with many communist states. Arab states might funnel money to the PLO, but they have not been eager to see the PLO gain real power over real territory.

Even in the heady months of personal triumph in 1974, Arafat could not control warring factions within the PLO, or prevent international terrorist raids by Palestinian radicals. Only six days after his UN speech, Palestinian terrorists killed four people in Israel. While Arafat might wave an olive branch, the deadly struggle between fedayeen and Israelis lurched along unchecked.

Yet by 1974, two things had happened that changed the political landscape of the Middle East. A 1973 war and a potent new Arab weapon—oil—had altered the balance of power. The resilient Arafat scrambled along a slippery tightrope in a volatile new political situation.

AFTER THE YOM KIPPUR WAR—
NEW REALISM

A year before Arafat appeared at the UN, Egypt, Syria, and Iraq attacked Israel on Yom Kippur, the most solemn day of the Jewish religious year. Though they lost the war, Arab armies at first captured some ground in the Golan Heights and Sinai Peninsula, putting to rest the idea that the Israeli armed forces were unbeatable.

Suddenly, the Arab states brandished a weapon that seemed as potent as bombs—petroleum. The oil-producing states of the Organization of Petroleum Exporting Countries (OPEC) cut off oil shipments to the United States and reduced shipments to Europe in protest against Western support for Israel in the war. Oil prices in the West doubled, and then doubled again. Oil shortages and skyrocketing oil prices shook the world's economy, and forced Europe and the United States to pay more heed to Arab interests. OPEC's weapon tilted the world power balance by giving new weight to conservative, oil-rich regimes like Saudi Arabia, which supported the PLO. The Persian Gulf oil states set aside some of their increased oil profits for the PLO.

Alan Hart, Arafat's authorized biographer, calls the Yom Kippur War a turning point in PLO fortunes. He says it gave Arafat the freedom he had wanted "to continue the struggle by political means."[2] After the Yom Kippur War, with Arab armies in total defeat, Arafat and other more practical voices tried to bring new realism into the PLO. When the Palestine National Council met in 1973, Farouq Qaddumi of Fatah said it was time to think about accepting the reality of Israel's existence, and time for the PLO to consider a Palestinian mini-state consisting of Gaza and the West Bank. The idea of being satisfied with only part of Palestine outraged Habash and other radicals, but Arafat began an exhaustive effort to bring them around. Over the next five years, Arafat says, he met personally with every member of the 300-person PNC, lobbying them to accept compromise and a mini-state of Palestine. The PNC adopted the idea in principle in 1977.

Arafat talked endlessly, arguing that diplomacy was a more promising way to gain a Palestinian state than warfare. These efforts to use words instead of guns split the PLO in 1974. On the one side was Fatah; on the other, the radicals, including those in groups dominated by Arab countries.

Another spinoff from Habash's group, the Democratic Front for the Liberation of Palestine (DFLP), sided with Arafat and Fatah. The DFLP was started by Nayef Hawatmeh, who much earlier had helped Habash found the PFLP. As time passed, Hawatmeh found himself favoring a more practical approach than Habash. Hawatmeh spoke up early in favor of a "mini-state" for the West Bank and Gaza.

Several radical groups in 1974 joined to form a Rejection Front, which "rejected" any approach other than the liberation of all Palestine. With the backing of Libya, Iraq, and other hard-line Arab countries, the Rejectionists favored armed struggle, not diplomacy. At the time it was founded, the Rejection Front consisted of the following groups, though the makeup changed as some groups reformed and renamed themselves:

- *The Popular Front for the Liberation of Palestine (PFLP),* headed by George Habash
- *The Popular Front for the Liberation of Palestine— General Command,* formed by Ahmed Jibril, who

earlier helped Habash found the PFLP, but broke away to form a separate group with Syrian backing in 1968
- *The Arab Liberation Front,* formed by Iraq in 1969 to counter the Syrian-backed Saiqa fedayeen group
- *The Popular Struggle Front,* another pro-Syrian organization, also known as the Palestinian Popular Struggle Front (PPSF)

Though it opposed Arafat and his allies, the Rejection Front did not walk out of the PLO. One who did was Sabri Khalil al-Banna, better known as Abu Nidal, who left Fatah to set up his own terrorist organization in Iraq. Abu Nidal swore to murder any Fatah member who opened talks with Israel.

Arafat also differed with radicals on how to deal with King Hussein. Many Palestinians still lived in Jordan, and Arafat wanted to work out deals to improve their lives. Jordan paid for some social services for Palestinians in the West Bank, even though it was occupied by Israel. Arafat thought Fatah should seek friendlier relations with the king, and he opened quiet talks with Jordan on various issues. Habash, whose model was Fidel Castro's revolution in Cuba, called for the king's overthrow. By 1974, however, such differences were overshadowed by peace efforts in the Middle East.

THE TREACHEROUS ROAD TO PEACE

At the time of the Rabat conference, a long effort to work out a Middle East peace was underway between Egypt, Israel, and the United States. Under U.S. pressure, Israel agreed to negotiate, even if PLO people were included. Issuing statements that could be read several ways, the PLO refused, saying the PLO covenant did not allow its representatives to recognize Israel. (Ironically, by 1990, these positions had been reversed: the PLO offered to talk, but Israel refused until the PLO could prove that it had renounced terrorism.)

Habash threatened to sabotage any international conference based on UN Resolution 242, which calls for recognition of secure boundaries for every state in the area, and therefore implies Israel's right to exist. Resolution 242 also speaks of a "just settlement of the refugee problem," rather than a return to their land by Palestinians. For these reasons, all factions within the PLO in the 1970s rejected Resolution 242 as a basis for settling the Palestine question.

While they debated tactics, PLO leaders watched with dismay as Egypt and Israel made a deal without them. In 1978, U.S. President Jimmy Carter achieved the seemingly impossible: he brought the leaders of Egypt and Israel together at the presidential retreat at Camp David in Maryland and got them to agree to a peace treaty. Signing for Egypt, President Anwar Sadat accepted the right of Israel to exist. In exchange, Israel returned the Sinai peninsula to Egypt. For his peace efforts, Sadat won the Nobel Peace Prize (along with Menachem Begin), but he infuriated his Arab neighbors. The Arab League promptly expelled Egypt.

The Camp David accords promised Palestinians a "self-governing authority" on the West Bank and Gaza; how it was to be governed was to be decided later by Israel, Jordan, and Egypt. Arafat charged that Sadat had sold out the Palestinians. Habash called for the Egyptian's assassination.

Camp David was to be a first step toward a broader Middle East peace, but the process stalled. A new government in Israel seemed uninterested in further peace talks, and in Lebanon, PLO forces, Syrians, and Israelis took sides in a widening civil war.

THE PLO IN LEBANON

When Jordan expelled the PLO in the early 1970s, Lebanon's fragile government was too weak to keep the fedayeen out. Tens of thousands of Palestinians joined those already living in Lebanon. By 1975, some 400,000 Palestinians made up about 20 percent of the Lebanese population. Most of them lived in Southern Lebanon, a region so thick with Palestinians that it was nicknamed Fatahland.

At first, Lebanese Muslims welcomed the arrival of the PLO as fellow Muslims who would protect them from right-wing Christian militia. However, young fedayeen with guns tended to strut around like the villains in western movies, bullying anyone in sight. Armed fedayeen drove some Lebanese from their homes and villages, and moved in behind them. As the PLO dug in, built fortifications, and stockpiled weapons, they also attracted Israeli attacks, attacks which injured Lebanese as well as Palestinians. The PLO therefore began to lose some of its Lebanese Muslim support.

In the twelve years from 1970 to 1982, the PLO in Lebanon took on more and more of the trappings of a government. The Palestine Red Crescent Organization, the Palestinian version of the Red Cross, ran clinics and hospitals. Headed by Arafat's brother, Dr. Fathi Arafat, by 1980 the Red Crescent operated nine hospitals in Lebanon plus twelve camp clinics. Palestinian students attended regular schools, but they also attended classes in Palestine culture and history run by the PLO. The PLO sponsored a variety of social and cultural organizations in the camps, and offered university scholarships. A group called Tiger Cubs trained boys between the ages of nine and fifteen to become fedayeen. At age twelve, boys who did well were sent away to six weeks of summer camp, some in communist countries of Eastern Europe, at PLO expense. PLO policemen patrolled the camps and PLO courts meted out justice. In its strongholds in the south, the PLO trained terrorists from around the world. Critics charged that the PLO of the 1970s ran a school for world terrorists in Lebanon— financed in part by the communist bloc.

By the mid-1970s, Arafat was being treated like a head of state, meeting diplomats from many countries. He was the first foreign leader invited to visit Iran after a revolution there installed the Ayatollah Khomeini as its leader.

"His was no longer a humble revolutionary movement, but rather a vigorous para-state, with a growing bureaucracy administering the affairs of Palestinians everywhere, and with a budget bigger than that of many small sovereign states,"[3] according to Rashid Khalidi, a Palestinian professor of political science at the University of Chicago. Khalidi's views are particularly interesting because he was teaching in Beirut during Lebanon's civil war.

The Palestinian "government in exile" established its headquarters in the Fakhani quarter of Beirut, in a complex of offices and bureaus. The neighborhood already had a Palestinian flavor because many middle-class Palestinians had settled there as early as 1948. At the Arab University in the quarter, most of the students were Palestinians. The PLO-sponsored Palestine Research Center and Institute of Palestinian Studies were in Beirut, creating both propaganda and research about Palestinians. Nearby, the big Sabra and Shattila refugee camps housed thousands of Palestinians. By the mid-1970s, therefore, Beirut was not only the headquarters of the PLO: It was the political, cultural, financial, and administrative capital for Palestinians.

As the PLO flexed its growing power, many Lebanese reacted with unease, but the government was too divided to clamp down. Lebanese society had split into bitterly opposed religious and political groups. Rivalries between right-wing Christians and Muslims, and between right-wing and leftist Muslims, made Lebanon all but ungovernable by 1975. Each side fielded small, quick-triggered armies. Armed bands fought one another on the streets. Looting, sniper fire, kidnapping, and assassinations by all sides marked Lebanon's spiral into chaos. PLO raids into Israel drew Israeli attacks, adding another heavily armed element to the tinderbox that was Lebanon.

In 1973, an Israeli raid on Beirut killed three Palestinian leaders, starting a chain reaction of warfare in which it was hard to keep up with who was fighting whom, and what allies had switched sides recently. When Christian militia attacked PLO camps, PLO forces defended them, but Arafat tried to keep Fatah from siding too closely with any group and therefore being drawn into open warfare. Groups of Palestinians lined up with opposing sides among the Lebanese factions. Fatah generally sided with right-wing Lebanese Muslims. The revolutionary governments of Syria and Iraq both equipped Palestinian commandos who fought in Lebanon. In general, Palestinian radicals fought on whatever side Syria and Iraq were backing at the moment.

Nineteen months of savage civil war and violence began in April 1975. The war was marked by brutality on all sides. During 1975 and early 1976, Syrian forces backed the PLO, but later turned against them and sided with Lebanese Christians and the Israelis.

Fatah eventually found it impossible to keep out of the fight. In support of its Muslim Lebanese allies, PLO heavy artillery pounded Christian-controlled areas of East Beirut. Arafat worked feverishly to get the warring sides to sign a cease-fire, fearing that fedayeen camps would be destroyed in all-out war.

Brutality reached new levels after a force of about 8,000 Palestinians in a Syrian-controlled fedayeen group called Saiga devastated the mostly Christian town of Damour, raping the women and killing some 6,000 people. After the attacks, the PLO moved into Damour in force, and the village became a large Palestinian settlement. In revenge for the massacre at Damour, Lebanese Christian militia surrounded and laid siege to a heavily populated Palestinian district of Beirut. They trapped some 30,000 people in Tel al-Zaatar for months, pounding the camp with heavy guns. Both sides claim the other committed atrocities. The PLO charges the Christian militia with a massacre after the district fell. The Lebanese Christians say the PLO shot residents who tried to flee during the siege.

Arafat was out of the country in 1976 when Syria switched sides and sent 30,000 troops to support Christian Lebanese forces attacking the PLO. It took him several weeks to smuggle himself back in, wearing a disguise, aboard an Egyptian corn ship. While he was gone, his second in command, Khalaf, ordered the PLO to fight the Syrians, a move Arafat had worked desperately to avoid. As fighting raged out of control, Arafat sent frantic messages to the king of Saudi Arabia urging him to press for a cease-fire.

The 1975–76 civil war ended in October 1976, when Arafat met with the presidents of Lebanon, Syria, and Egypt to agree to a cease-fire. The PLO promised not to interfere in Lebanon's internal affairs. The cease-fire left Syrian troops dug in throughout the central and northern parts of a ruined country that was split into zones controlled by Syrians, Maronite Christians, and Lebanese Muslims. The Israelis held much of the south, and the PLO hung on to some pockets of strength. From these spots, the PLO continued to raid across the Israeli border into Galilee.

In March 1978, eight Fatah commandos led by an eighteen-year-old woman hijacked an Israeli bus. In the shootout that followed, thirty-seven people, many of them children, were killed. In response, Israel invaded Lebanon to attack PLO refugee camps with 25,000 troops supported by aircraft and naval landing craft. The massive attack destroyed several Lebanese villages and killed 700 Palestinians. Palestinians and their Muslim Lebanese allies fled north. By PLO estimates, at least half a million people evacuated their homes and took refuge in Sidon, Beirut, and elsewhere.

The United Nations sent a peace-keeping force, and Arafat agreed that the PLO would abide by the cease-fire lines. Helena Cobban, who has written one of the most balanced histories of the PLO, says this was the first time the PLO had openly agreed to a cease-fire with Israel, and that Arafat's decision to cooperate with the United Nations force was later endorsed by all PLO groups.[4] According to Cobban, in the following months, Arafat proved himself able to keep his part of the bargain. He took ruthless action against Palestinian elements, including some in Fatah, who tried to violate the cease-fire. Fatah special police arrested renegade fedayeen who tried to undermine the cease-fire.

One PLO official, Abu Kifah, has compared those years to playing the Pac Man video game.[5] There were battles to fight everywhere, with the bug popping up randomly and repeatedly. No sooner did one battle end than another erupted elsewhere in an unexpected place.

The PLO had lost territory again, but as the fedayeen retreated, the PLO attracted many new recruits among Palestinians living elsewhere. A number of fedayeen left the Syrian-backed Saiqa to sign up with Fatah, which seemed more devoted to Palestinian, and less to Syrian, causes. The remaining PLO stronghold, Beirut, became a prime Israeli target.

BEIRUT: SIEGE AND EVACUATION

Once a beautiful and prosperous capital city, Beirut in 1981 had split into two damaged and heavily armed war zones: Christian East Beirut and Muslim West Beirut. For a Christian to enter the Muslim sector or a Muslim to enter the Christian quarter was to risk a beating, rape, kidnapping, or murder. Brutal acts of violence were committed by all sides of this civil war—against PLO units, against Israelis, against the various Lebanese armies, against innocent civilians. In response to PLO attacks in Galilee, Israeli raids pounded West Beirut into a partial rubble. As part of a war of nerves, Israeli agents used car bombs to try to pick off top PLO leaders. In July 1981 Israel attacked PLO strongholds in West Beirut in a raid that killed 300 people. A week later, the PLO and Israel agreed to a cease-fire, but PLO terrorist raids continued to harass northern Israeli settlements.

Once again, Arafat tried to restrain the radicals. He warned that an all-out Israeli invasion was coming. He ordered stockpiles of food, weapons, and medicines against the expected attack. It came in June 1982, after Abu Nidal terrorists in London shot and injured an Israeli ambassador. The PLO promptly denied responsibility for the shooting, but the next day Israeli aircraft began shelling Palestinian refugee camps in Lebanon.

On June 6, 1982, some 90,000 Israeli forces entered Lebanon in a three-pronged attack backed up by Lebanese Christian militia. Israeli armored columns rumbled up the coast, leapfrogging PLO strongholds at Tyre, Sidon, and Damour, and barreling straight to Beirut. A second prong of the Israeli attack sent Israeli infantry to encircle PLO bases in the south, while a third force landed by sea north of Sidon.

Israelis had expected to overwhelm the refugee camps in Fatahland in the south quickly, but they met fierce resistance in the rugged terrain. At a camp outside of Tyre, an Israeli division of more than 10,000 pounded the camp for nearly four days before the PLO resistance collapsed. The Palestinian camp of Ain al-Hilweh held out for ten days. Many of those fighting were young Tiger Cubs who stood their ground alongside adults against the Israelis.

The massive attacks on Palestinian strongholds badly damaged the cities of Tyre and Sidon. After their collapse, some 50,000 Palestinians fled north, crowding Beirut even more.

Looking back, Arafat said proudly that the PLO fighters held out longer than any Arab army had in any previous war with Israel. For more than seven weeks, Israeli aircraft and heavy artillery pounded West Beirut, where the PLO had its headquarters. Israeli bombs leveled several apartment buildings believed to house one or more PLO leaders. The Israelis cut off electric service, food, and water to the besieged city. Many civilian deaths occurred, largely because the PLO deliberately put heavy artillery in and around schools, hospitals, and other places where an Israeli attack would harm innocent people and thus cause outrage in the outside world. Israelis charge that the PLO deliberately and callously put civilians in jeopardy.

During the seige, Arafat seemed to be everywhere, touring the front line, talking to fedayeen troops, visiting the wounded in hospitals. Al-Wazir directed most of the military actions, while Khalaf headed efforts to rally fedayeen and civilian resistance.

As the siege wore on, the United States tried to work out a cease-fire. After the United States guaranteed the safety of Palestinians who would remain in Lebanon, the PLO agreed to withdraw from Beirut and hand over its heavy artillery to the Lebanese army. Between August 21 and September 1, some 11,000 guerrillas left

*An emotional Arafat addresses his officers in 1982 at a
farewell gathering in West Beirut,
as the PLO begins to withdraw from Lebanon.*

Lebanon by land and sea. Arafat was evacuated on August 30 by ship to Athens, Greece.

After PLO forces were no longer on hand to protect the camps, Lebanese Christian militia entered the Palestinian refugee camps of Sabra and Shattila in an area controlled by the Israeli army. For forty-two hours, the militia rampaged through the camps, killing more than 700 men, women, and children, and in some cases mutilating the bodies. Israeli soldiers on duty outside the camps had orders not to interfere or to enter the camps. After the massacre, the PLO felt betrayed by the United States, which had guaranteed the safety of Palestinian civilians.

Once again, Arafat and the PLO had been driven from their headquarters. They had been forced from Palestine, from Jordan, and now from Lebanon. A sensible forecaster might have said the PLO was down for the count, and many did say so. Palestinians now had no real base, no headquarters. Many in the PLO inner circle thought it was time to change leadership as well.

CHAPTER 7

REVOLT AND A STALLED PEACE EFFORT (1982–87)

As his ship left the rubble of Beirut behind in 1982, Yasir Arafat and the PLO looked beaten. The PLO's state-within-a-state in Lebanon was shattered, its military forces crushed and scattered. Yet five years later, Arafat had engineered a remarkable comeback, and he had dragged a reluctant PLO into new peace talks. These efforts to work for a diplomatic solution instead of a military one nearly cost him the PLO leadership.

The PLO that evacuated from Beirut in 1982 had split into three main camps. One was Arafat's Fatah, or at least the shrinking remnants of Fatah still loyal to him after the disaster in Lebanon. A second large element rallied around Habash and the PFLP, and called for all-out social revolution and armed struggle. A third, newly powerful group included anti-Arafat radicals and terrorists backed by Syria, Iraq, and Libya. The Arab governments backing the radicals had their own hopes of controlling Palestine.

Arafat had to decide where to rebuild the PLO's

headquarters operation. He chose Tunis, the capital of the North African state Tunisia, 2,000 miles (3,200 km) from Palestine. The Arab League's headquarters, at that time, was in Tunis, making it a natural meeting ground for diplomats of the Arab nations.

Many Fatah supporters followed Arafat to Tunisia, but Fatah also wanted a military base in a frontline state bordering Israel. Fedayeen were eager to fight; Fatah needed bases for commandos. If it was to keep its leadership of the PLO, Fatah had to hang on to the footholds it controlled in Lebanon despite the thousands of Syrian and Israeli troops patrolling there.

As they rebuilt, Arafat and his top aides lived like fugitives, moving in unpredictable patterns and trying not to pause in one spot long enough for assassins to reach them. They were hunted by agents of both Israel's Mossad and Palestinian terror groups. Arab radicals cursed Arafat as a traitor because he was willing to talk about a Palestinian mini-state and about making peace with Israel. He and his aides never moved without heavy guards. Yet despite their precautions, the Abu Nidal and other terror groups killed several PLO officials who were working for a diplomatic settlement with Israel and Jordan. Between 1973 and 1989, the Abu Nidal group alone murdered at least eleven PLO officials, including one who was Abu Nidal's nephew.[1]

Nothing in the Middle East is ever simple, and between 1982 and 1985, several complex chains of events whipsawed the PLO. One involved U.S. efforts to restart the Middle East peace process. Another was Syria's drive to eliminate Arafat and take control of the PLO. The Syrian effort dovetailed with a Fatah revolt against Arafat and a challenge to his chairmanship of the PLO. Lastly, there were Arafat's talks with Jordan about a possible deal for joint control of Palestine.

As Arafat left Beirut in 1982, the sluggish peace process between Egypt, the United States, and Israel came to life again. President Ronald Reagan put forward a peace plan that reopened the debate. The stakes had changed, however, since the 1970s. Many more Jewish settlers had moved into the West Bank. In 1981 Israel announced that it was turning the West Bank and Gaza (ruled since 1967 by the military) over to a civilian administration. Palestinians saw the move as a step toward Israeli annexation.

Israelis hoped to deal with King Hussein of Jordan in working out a permanent solution to the problem of the Palestinians. Even though he had agreed in 1974 that the PLO was the legitimate representative of Palestinians, Hussein still treated the West Bank as an extension of Jordan. He paid the salaries of some civil servants, and issued Jordanian passports to people who wanted to travel.

That was the situation in 1982 when President Reagan tossed out a new version of the "land for peace" idea. Israel would withdraw from most lands taken in 1967 in exchange for recognition by Arab nations and a formal peace treaty. Reagan also spoke of self-government by the Palestinians of the West Bank and Gaza in association with Jordan. To work out the details, the United States suggested an international conference based on UN Resolution 242. (See Appendix) Prime Minister Menachem Begin of Israel rejected the proposals outright, vowing never to give up one inch of the occupied territories.

Meanwhile, at an Arab summit meeting in Fez, Morocco, that same year, the Arab nations dusted off a plan proposed earlier by King Fahd of Saudi Arabia.

The Fez summit called for the United Nations to guarantee peace among all states in the region, and said the PLO should have a key role in any negotiations.

Though not sure whether to support the Reagan moves or not, Arafat met with King Hussein to see if there might be a way to agree on some sort of joint Jordanian-Palestinian administration in Palestine. To PLO radicals, Arafat sold out the moment he met with their old enemy, the king of Jordan.

On April 4, 1983, the PLO executive council rejected Arafat's efforts to work with Jordan. Six days later, an Abu Nidal terrorist assassinated Jordan's representative to the peace talks. The king withdrew from the talks and said it was up to Palestinians "to determine the course of their action to save themselves and their land."

REVOLT SPLITS PLO

All this cozying up to the old enemy, King Hussein, and hinting of peace with Israel outraged Palestinian hotheads in and out of the PLO. Shortly after Reagan announced his peace plan, the massacre of Palestinians at Sabra and Shattila in Lebanon sharpened the sense of rage and betrayal among Palestinians. The massacre drove some elements of the PLO further into the radical camp that vowed revenge, war, revolution, and no compromises—ever. While Arafat made warlike speeches and public statements, privately he urged flexibility and diplomacy. Not surprisingly, radicals called him soft, a compromiser, unfit for leadership of a fighting organization. The unity Arafat had worked so long to build collapsed.

President Hafez Assad of Syria fanned the radical unrest. Assad nursed ambitions to dominate not only Syria but Lebanon and Palestine as well. He therefore used the split within the PLO to promote his own goals. Assad made no secret of his opinion that Arafat was a small-time politico out of his depth in world affairs. While he ridiculed Arafat, Assad plotted to put his own supporters, members of Saiqa, into the top PLO spots. Since the PLO's main fedayeen centers were in Syria and Lebanon, Assad was in a very strong position to dictate terms. He happened to have 40,000 Syrian troops stationed in Lebanon, more than enough to crush any PLO military challenge to him. Just to confuse things further, Iraq also equipped fedayeen who opposed Arafat as President Saddam Hussein nursed his own ambitions to dominate the entire region.

The losers in most wars quarrel bitterly about who was responsible for the loss. The fedayeen remaining in Lebanon quarreled violently, with words, fists, and guns. Some Fatah troops questioned the military leadership of Arafat and Abu Jihad during the fight in Beirut. Local Fatah commanders ignored directives sent them from Tunis. Assad kept the discontent boiling by supplying arms and money to Syrian-controlled fedayeen in key positions.

In 1983, elements of Fatah in Lebanon broke openly with Arafat and lined up with Assad. One of the rebel leaders, Saed Musa, had served as Arafat's military adviser only a year earlier. Musa resigned from the PLO and formed his own fighting group, Fatah Uprising.

Though forces loyal to him were vastly outnumbered, Arafat slipped back into Lebanon to direct Fatah fedayeen who were protecting refugee camps. He set up headquarters in the northern city of Tripoli. In a direct challenge to Arafat's prestige, Syrian-backed forces attacked the refugee camps and Tripoli. Arafat commanded fewer than 5,000 loyal Fatah forces as he battled Abu Musa and other rebels. Syria backed Abu Musa with Soviet tanks and weapons, plus thousands of regular Syrian troops. The Syrian forces trapped Arafat's Fatah fighters along the coast. Once again, Arafat had to flee Lebanon.

Two assassination attempts failed as Arafat left Tripoli. Still, his enemies thought they had finally broken his hold on the PLO. Two days later Arafat confounded his critics—and infuriated the Fatah inner circle, which had not known what he planned—by appearing publicly with the Egyptian president, Hosni Mubarak. Egypt was still an outcast in the Arab world, yet here was Arafat publicly greeting the Egyptian leader. PLO rebels reacted with outrage to Arafat's showy gesture. They warned Arab governments to have no further dealings with Arafat. George Habash of the PFLP joined Fatah rebels in demanding the ouster of Arafat as PLO chairman.

While such quarrels weakened the leadership, PLO military forces in 1983 were so broken and scattered that they no longer posed a serious threat to Israel. None of the frontline states bordering Israel allowed fedayeen groups to operate freely. Assad kept tight reins on fedayeen operating from Syria. Israeli troops patrolled southern Lebanon, making it difficult for PLO guerrillas to attack from the north. Seemingly, Arafat's room for maneuvering had run out.

ARAFAT REGAINS CONTROL

Assad's representatives quietly approached Salah Khalaf and Khalad al-Hassan in turn, offering each the chairmanship of the PLO if he would oppose Arafat; both refused. In a round of nonstop talking, persuading, and arm-twisting, Arafat slowly won back the support of enough people to risk a showdown. At the 1984 meeting of the Palestine National Council, challengers tried to unseat him. Faced with volleys of criticism in the opening days, Arafat dramatically resigned as chairman. No one else even began to have enough support to replace him. Within hours, a parade of visitors begged him to reconsider. When the dust settled, Arafat was again chairman, and the PNC agreed to endorse his negotiations with King Hussein. However, the radicals who opposed him in 1983 remained a noisy, disruptive—and often murderous— minority opposed to peace talks with Israel. They continued to sabotage every serious move to achieve a lasting peace.

After two years of off-and-on talks, in 1985 Arafat and Hussein agreed to a joint negotiating strategy with Israel. They left the exact outlines deliberately vague, but Arafat may have agreed to the idea of a Palestinian state in a loose federation with Jordan. When Hussein first floated the federation idea in 1972, the PLO had rejected it totally. However, the approach has always had supporters in Israel. About 60 percent of Jordan's population is Palestinian (the rest is mostly Bedouin). Therefore, some arrangement involving Jordan seemed to many people to make sense. On the other hand, some factions in Israel use the slogan, "Jordan *is* Palestine," meaning Jordan is the logical homeland for any exiled Palestinians needing a home. Such a solution would leave the West Bank and Gaza for Israel, and therefore is not acceptable to most Palestinians.

Despite the 1985 agreement, the talks between Jordan and the PLO sputtered to an end without agreement. In 1986 King Hussein said he was giving up the effort. He stated he would deal directly with Israel, thus leaving the PLO on the outside again.

While the leaders talked, a newspaper polled Palestinians in the territories in the summer of 1986. The poll showed that 93 percent of the population wanted a Palestinian state under the PLO. Seventy-one percent favored a state headed by Arafat; only 3 percent would choose King Hussein.[2]

"I WANT SOMETHING FOR OUR PEOPLE"

Why did Arafat agree to peace plans he had rejected twenty years earlier? Shortly before he and Hussein reached agreement on joint tactics in 1985, Arafat chatted with Edward Said, an American scholar who is a Palestinian and a member of the PNC. Arafat reminded Said of the 1940s and 1950s, when the Mufti of Jerusalem refused to accept an Israeli state or to compromise in any way. "Haj Amin was pure and he never made concessions," Arafat told Said. "I don't want to be another Haj Amin. He got us nothing. I want something for our people."[3]

This practical goal seemingly began to guide Arafat's actions. As a younger man, he acted and sounded much more radical, and he vowed to fight forever. Then a certain realism seemed to have set in. He saw time trickling out as a third generation of Palestinians was born in the crowded refugee camps. By the mid-1980s, he was willing to deal, talk, and double-talk and compromise with anyone who might help win the Palestinians some land of their own. For the same reasons, Arafat declared in Cairo in 1985 that he renounced terror. At least, he renounced what he defined as terror. He pledged not to support international terror, but said Fatah would continue to strike Israeli "military targets." Arafat knew that no settlement was possible in the Middle East conflict without U.S. involvement. President Reagan said repeatedly that the United States would not press

Israel to deal with the PLO as long as the PLO supported terrorists.

From the Israeli viewpoint, of course, the PLO always was a terrorist group, and continued to be one. Major acts of terrorism by Palestinians not under Arafat's direct control stiffened the Israeli government's determination to keep the PLO out of any talks about the West Bank and Gaza. American opinion also hardened in 1985 when an Abu Nidal operation captured the cruise ship *Achille Lauro*. During the takeover, terrorists shot and killed an elderly American Jewish man in a wheelchair and then pushed him overboard. Both Americans and Israelis have pointed out that the man who planned the hijacking, Mohammed Abbas (Abul Abbas), sits on the PLO executive committee representing the Palestine Liberation Front. Arafat knew that such actions were disasters for the Palestinian cause, yet he seemed unwilling to risk a showdown to expel more radical elements from the PLO.

Throughout the diplomatic maneuvering of the 1980s, the PLO continued to attack Israel and Israel continued to strike back. Israelis bombed PLO headquarters outside Tunis in 1985, and managed to damage the apartment where Arafat was staying. He happened to be at Abu Jihad's house, and so again escaped harm.

Once more Arafat had survived, to emerge as the single dominant voice in the PLO. He pressed harder for diplomatic solutions to the now forty-year-old problem of Palestine. Arafat told an interviewer in 1987:

". . . We have two options: to continue in this very tough military confrontation between us and them, or to find the solution through the United Nations, and this means the international conference, to achieve a lasting and permanent solution to the Middle East crisis."[4]

Observers questioned whether this diplomatic effort

Meeting with Egyptian president Hosni Mubarak in 1985. The meeting ended an uncomfortable diplomatic isolation of the Palestinian leader following the Achille Lauro *hijacking and killing of an American by Palestinian gunmen.*

was aboveboard, and whether the PLO and Arafat would ever actually accept Israel's right to exist. Yet the diplomatic efforts stumbled forward, however erratically, spurred by the population explosion in the occupied territories.

CHAPTER 8

THE INTIFADA

Beit Sahur is a West Bank town of about 11,000 people that made headlines with a slogan from the American Revolution. The town's business and factory owners stopped paying taxes, saying they were no longer willing to pay the costs of an occupying army. Speaking for the town, the mayor declared, "No taxation without representation." West Bank Palestinians are taxed by Israel, but are not citizens and so cannot vote to elect the Israeli government.

Faced with a town-wide tax revolt, Israel sent tax collectors backed by soldiers to Beit Sahur. Since they couldn't collect in money, the Israelis gathered up goods from tax delinquents, and hauled away everything from VCRs and furniture to food and factory machinery. From Asya Hanna Khier's small wood-carving shop, for instance, they confiscated the Christian crosses and figurines he sells to Christian pilgrims (Beit Sahur is near Bethlehem). From a small factory, they took the sewing machines.

Beit Sahur is somewhat unusual in the West Bank

because most of its residents are middle-class Christians. Many West Bank people are poorer, and most are Muslim. The decision by Beit Sahur's solid citizens not to pay Israeli taxes underscored the unity that the Intifada, or uprising, had forged among Palestinians in the West Bank and Gaza. A mass movement with enormous grass-roots support, the Intifada had upended daily life in the occupied territories. Every day Palestinians in the territories demonstrated their hatred of Israeli occupation, and every day they paid a heavy toll for their rebellion.

Schools in Beit Sahur closed for most of two academic years because Israeli authorities viewed them as breeding grounds for unrest. Most Gaza schools stayed open. In the seething West Bank, however, when authorities reopened the elementary and secondary schools, they soon shut them again after more violence occurred. When Israelis closed the regular schools, parents and the PLO organized classes in basements and homes for elementary and secondary students. After more incidents of stone throwing, Israeli patrols shut down the underground schools as well.

Israel reopened most elementary and secondary schools in July 1989 and sixteen community colleges in 1990, but decided to keep the five West Bank universities closed. Some students still managed to attend classes. At Bir Zeit University in Ramallah, students hid their books in bags of groceries or other disguises and slipped to classes at professors' homes and other meeting places. Kuwait's government supplied the money to pay professors and buy books.

Palestinians considered themselves the best-educated people of the Arab world, and they placed a very high value on education. The loss of schooling had therefore been a costly price to pay for rebellion. Palestinians also paid an economic toll for their uprising. Family incomes dropped 40 to 50 percent in the first year after the uprising began. Despite the sacrifices, the Intifada had deep-rooted support among the 1.7 million Palestinians of the occupied territories. They vowed to continue it as long as Israel holds the West Bank and Gaza.

Since the uprising began in December 1987, Israel had been able to contain and, to some extent, control the Intifada, but it had not been able to end it. Symbols of revolt appeared everywhere. PLO flags flew in defiance of Israeli military orders, and PLO and nationalist slogans blanketed walls and fences. Israeli patrols ordered the flags torn down and the slogans painted over, but after the troops left, new flags went up, and new slogans appeared overnight. Even wearing a kaffiyeh scarf or the national colors of red, black, green, and white was a gesture of defiance. A candy store owner in Nablus named his two daughters Palestine and Liberation.

A group of international political scientists happened to be in Israel to study the effects of Israeli occupation on the West Bank and Gaza just months after the Intifada started. Middle East authority Don Peretz said the group found that the Intifada "was having an enduring political, social and economic impact, not only on Arab-Jewish relations within the territories, but throughout Israeli society." Peretz noted that the Intifada arose not only out of the Palestinians' bitterness over their daily lives, but also from their "feelings of abandonment by the outside world, particularly by their Arab brethren."[1]

The Intifada, in other words, was homegrown. It wasn't imported by outsiders. The revolt was born in Palestine and was kept boiling by people who lived there. The Palestinians did, however, get a lot of help from the PLO.

The spark that set off the Intifada was outrage over the killing of four Palestinians by an Israeli military truck in Gaza. Wild rumors flashed through Gaza that Israelis were killing Palestinians. Groups of high school and college students surged into the streets, hurling rocks and shouting anti-Israeli slogans. Rioting spread to the West Bank. When the army was sent to stop the riots, Palestinians pelted the troops with stones, an action that became the Intifada's trademark.

The riots uncorked pent-up anger and despair built up over twenty years of Israeli occupation since the 1967 war. People vowed to keep on being troublemakers, to keep demonstrating until something changed. Daily acts of defiance helped create bonds of solidarity between villages and towns, and among Palestinians of all ages in the territories. The uprising also forced both the PLO and Israel to rethink their positions.

THE SHEBAB AND THE PLO

In many ways, the Intifada was a youth crusade. Students began it, and youths between the ages of ten and twenty supplied most of its infantry. A Beit Sahur schoolteacher explained ruefully: "I admit we are committing suicide, but we cannot retreat. Our children want an end to the occupation and they are running the show. What are we going to tell them, we don't want independence? I would be degraded in the eyes of my children if I told them to stop."[2]

Israelis arrested hundreds of Beit Sahur youths, and hundreds more throughout the 424 villages and towns of the West Bank. The young rebels hurling most of the stones were part of the *shebab*, which means "the guys." They belonged to a loosely organized "Popular Army" that replaced regular police in the occupied territories. After the uprising began, the underground PLO leadership ordered Palestinians to resign from the Israeli-run police forces. The shebab replaced them.

Wearing ski masks or kaffiyehs to mask their faces,

Children demonstrate with Palestinian
flags and balloons on the
first anniversary of the Intifada—
the Palestinian uprising.

the shebab prowled the streets, alleys, and outskirts of towns and villages. They were part vigilantes, part street gang. Shebab youths harassed and beat up people found dealing drugs or committing crimes. However, their main mission was taunting Israeli patrols. When someone— usually a girl in a lookout window—spotted soldiers, shrill whistles filled the air, alerting the shebab. Masked youths pelted soldiers and military vehicles with stones, or sometimes threw Molotov cocktails (gasoline bombs). The youths heaped up tires and set them afire to create smoky roadblocks against Israeli patrols. The shebab and older Palestinians sometimes also attacked Jewish settlers on the West Bank. These attacks led to some of the most bloody confrontations of the uprising, and stirred bitter anger in Israel.

As the Intifada entered its third year, the Israeli Defense Ministry reported that 85 percent of the violent activity was stone throwing, including the throwing of huge boulders; that 60 percent of that was done by children thirteen or younger. These were young people who had grown up under occupation. They had lived their entire lives as stateless people with few civil rights, a situation that bred an outraged sense of frustrated helplessness. The Intifada offered them a mission, an exciting way to act out their rage and determination not to be ignored.

Initially caught by surprise by the Intifada, the exiled leadership of the PLO scrambled to gain control of it, and to use the Intifada to gain world attention and sympathy for the Palestinians. Before his death in 1988, Khalil al-Wazir (Abu Jihad) set up an underground network to funnel funds to the Intifada. He also created a secret committee to coordinate the uprising in the territories. Its leadership was a closely guarded secret, but the unified command was thought to consist of people from Fatah and three other PLO groups (the PFLP,

PDFLP, and the Palestinian Communist Party). Although the Israelis arrested several people believed to be part of the command group, the committee's operations went on without interruption.

Every two weeks or so, the underground leadership prepared leaflets that outlined tactics and gave directives for strikes, boycotts, demonstrations, and other actions. Before the leaflets were printed and distributed, drafts were faxed to PLO headquarters in Tunis for comment and suggestions.

Local organizations in every village and neighborhood spread the leaflets and tended to decide for themselves whether to follow orders. The shebab in Nablus, for instance, was organized into "shock committees" of ten to fifteen youths who patrolled every block of the town. They not only harassed Israelis who entered the town, they also tried to enforce the orders issued in biweekly leaflets of the underground united command.

Local committees also organized underground schools, strikes, food distribution, first aid, and medical care. The PLO funneled large sums of money into the West Bank and Gaza to support the uprising. PLO funds provided, among other things, money for families of people who were killed, pensions for widows, and medical treatment of wounded. By one estimate, the PLO spent at least $300 million in the territories within the first eighteen months of the uprising. PLO commands in Sidon and Tyre, Lebanon, were responsible for running supply lines by sea and land that brought food, clothing, medicine, and other supplies into the occupied territories.

Despite such activities, the PLO did not truly control the Intifada, and by the third year of the uprising, seemed to be losing influence to newer groups. With only limited success, Arafat and the PLO leadership warned repeatedly against killing Israelis, which invited harsh reprisals. Urging the shebab to limit themselves to nothing more lethal than rocks, the PLO told the youths to harass, not kill. The PLO said not to use guns or other "hot weapons" that kill Israelis. Yet the top leadership of the PLO were far away; people in the West Bank increasingly ignored the orders from afar, impatient with calls for calm and patience.

Arafat tried to channel protests into boycotts of Israeli goods, strikes that withheld Palestinian labor from Israel, and other less violent actions that helped improve the Palestinians' image. In such ways, the moderates hoped, Palestinians could gain world attention, isolate Israel, and gain sympathy for the Palestinian cause.

In urging mostly nonviolent forms of civil disobedience in the Intifada, the PLO found itself out of step with more militant Palestinians, and far from its origins as a fighting group. Many radicals scorned such mild forms of rebellion. As Israel continued to refuse to negotiate with the PLO, radicals turned more and more to violence and killing, ignoring the PLO.

Through nearly three years of rebellion, however, the normally argumentative Palestinians in the territories showed a rare unity. They vowed to keep the uprising going forever, if necessary. In the process, they drew rare international interest and sympathy for their cause. For the PLO, the Intifada became therefore both an opportunity and a great challenge to Arafat's leadership.

COLLABORATORS AND FUNDAMENTALISTS

While the uprising had great popular support, it also had a darker side that exposed the tradition of violence that shadowed the Middle East. Palestinians who opposed the Intifada or wanted to give up learned to keep silent. Shadowy groups terrorized people who spoke up or who were suspected of cooperating with the Israelis. In the first two years of the uprising, some 250 people accused of aiding the Israelis were murdered, and the rate of murders increased as the third year began. By February of the third year of the uprising, more Palestinians were killed by Palestinians each month than by Israelis—despite repeated pleas from top PLO leaders not to carry out killings of collaborators without at least some sort of a trial or hearing.

Particular targets were people suspected of collaborating with Israel's security agency. Others were killed for selling land to Jews, for drug dealing, and for prostitution. Also among the victims were Palestinians chosen by Israel as mayors and other local officials in the territories. Ordered to resign from his post as a gesture of solidarity with the Intifada, Mayor Hassan al-Tawil of El Bireh stayed on, only to be stabbed by attackers. He still refused to quit, so militants set fire to his house. "People are being killed who are suspected of not being 100 percent supporters of the PLO line,"[3] he said on Israeli radio as he finally resigned.

The underground leadership tried to stem the terrorism and vigilante justice. One leaflet in August 1988, for instance, urged Palestinians not to kill other Arabs suspected of working with Israelis unless the killing had been authorized by an underground court. The "accepted" process of dealing with suspected collaborators was supposed to begin by informing an underground committee that someone was a suspect. The committee gathered information, often by having shebab follow the suspect's movements. If the evidence indicated the person was aiding Israel, one or two warnings were sent to the suspect's home. As a last step, in areas under PLO control, the evidence of collaboration was sent to Tunis for a verdict.

In many areas, however, the PLO lost control to newly powerful Muslim groups. Many of the killings in Gaza were the work of such groups. The most powerful of these organizations, Hamas, the Movement of Islamic Opposition, was widely believed to be a rebirth of the old Muslim Brotherhood. Like Haj Amin forty years earlier, Hamas preached a holy war to liberate Palestine. The organization was founded a month after the start of the Intifada, and drew massive support. Hamas called for no compromise with a Jewish state, and rejected any solution except the destruction of Israel. The organization also demanded that any Palestinian national state be based strictly on Islamic laws.

Hamas represented a powerful new Islamic rival to the more Westernized PLO. The PLO had no religious leaning, and included Muslims, Christians, communists, and atheists. By some estimates, as many as 80 percent of the Palestinians in Gaza, and about 40 percent in the West Bank belonged to Hamas. Other estimates put the Hamas membership lower, but by enforcing its orders with kidnapping and murders, Hamas intimidated many people into silence. A store owner in Bethlehem told a reporter that it didn't pay to fight the Hamas people, because they don't listen. "We are PLO here, but we're not going to get killed over this rivalry. Hamas is too strong."[4]

By the third year of the uprising, PLO leadership of the Intifada was challenged by a loose alliance of militant Islamic groups like Hamas and hard-liners and leftists in the PLO, led by Habash and the PFLP. Most deaths in the third year of the uprising were Palestinians killing Palestinians as radicals murdered people thought to be seeking peace or cooperating with Israel.

ISRAELI RESPONSE

Israelis outlawed Hamas, just as they made the PLO illegal in Israel and the territories. Israeli commanders said they were getting better at controlling the Intifada's violence. However, as one commander remarked, ''The essence of the Intifada is not in the actual level of activity but in the perception of the population . . . the sense of identity, direction and organization.''[5]

Measures to control the Intifada had solid support from the Israeli public. Israelis said they acted with restraint in the face of great provocation. They pointed out that since Palestinians had been dedicated for forty years to destroying Israel, Israel had no choice but to defend itself.

Israel had the only democratic government in the Middle East, the only one in which public policies were debated and voted upon by an elected legislature. Therefore, Israeli response to the Intifada was different from what might occur in an Arab land faced with a public rebellion. Most Arab rulers would simply use all the police or military force needed to crush a popular rebellion. Because of its strong democratic traditions and commitment to civil rights, Israel was not willing to use all the force at its command, but it used far more force than its critics think was wise or democratic.

Responsibility for controlling the uprising rested with the Defense Ministry, which used several riot-control measures. Tear gas broke up large gatherings. Troops made surprise sweeps and house-to-house searches, often after midnight, to find agitators. Homes of suspected agitators were blown up or bulldozed. When a whole community rioted, troops made mass arrests. Schools were closed to prevent young people from gathering. Frequent curfews kept people indoors. In some towns, the only public gatherings allowed were religious services.

The army had clearly defined limits on how much force soldiers were allowed to use. They had orders not to shoot children under thirteen or women. Troops were issued plastic and rubber bullets, which were less deadly than metal bullets. Soldiers had orders to use plastic bullets unless their lives were threatened. If they had to shoot, soldiers were supposed to aim for the legs. Despite such orders, in tense confrontations, shots were fired in confusion. Many women and children were shot and killed. (Many soldiers attacked and killed by Palestinians were teenagers.)

More than 900 Palestinians—most of them under twenty-five and some of them children—died since the Intifada began. During the same period, forty-two Israelis, including thirty-one civilians, were killed in the uprising. Some 15,000 to 20,000 Palestinians were wounded, and more than 50,000 arrested. Many of those jailed were not charged with a crime.

Though it controlled the uprising, Israel's Ministry of Defense warned the government that military steps would not end the Intifada; only a political solution would do so. "There is no such thing as eradicating the Intifada," the Israeli army chief of staff said in February 1989, "because in its essence it expresses the struggle of nationalism."[6]

Israel's leader, Prime Minister Yitzhak Shamir, however, rejected this view. "The populace will come to understand from the bitter experience of the Intifada violence that this struggle will lead nowhere and that everything the PLO stands for will produce only disasters. They will eventually grow disappointed with the Intifada and with the PLO. . . . I hope that will not take long,"[7] he said in October 1989.

Unless a government was willing to use ruthless methods, it was extremely difficult for an army to control a large and restless civilian population forever. Palestinians in the occupied territories believed they had numbers on their side. Some 1.7 million Palestinian Arabs lived under Israeli occupation as noncitizens in the West Bank and Gaza, and their population was growing very fast. Another 750,000 Arabs lived within Israel itself, and had Israeli citizenship. Israel's total Jewish population was about 3.5 million, of whom about 80,000 had settled in the West Bank.

TWO GIANT STEPS

The mass uprising that refused to die had several political results: 1) It caused King Hussein to give up Jordan's claims to the West Bank. 2) It shifted the focus of Palestinian issues to people living in what is called Palestine, rather than those in exile. 3) It forced the PLO to take actions it had rejected earlier—namely, accept Israel's right to exist, and renounce terrorism.

Eight months after the Intifada started, King Hussein said he would drop Jordan's claims to the West Bank. The king stopped paying salaries for civil servants and shut down government services in the West Bank. He challenged the PLO to take full responsibility for Palestinians.

Jordan's pull out put great pressure on the PLO to either take immediate political action in the occupied territories or stand aside and let the people living there work out their own future. Arafat no longer had the luxury of time to build unity among the PLO's quarreling branches. People in the West Bank and Gaza were boiling with an urgency to do something now, immediately, to gain a better future.

The crucial showdown for the PLO took place at a meeting of the Palestinian National Council in Algiers in November 1988. The PNC was forced at last to face the politically embarrassing truth that Palestinians probably would never get back all or even most of the original Palestine. Militants, of course, fought fiercely to prevent any such admission. Arafat went into nonstop motion, glad-handing and greeting everyone, calling even the most minor delegate by name. For instance, he hugged

*PLO chairman Arafat and other members
attending the Palestinian National
Council raise their hands, approving
the acceptance of the Palestinian
Communist party in the council.*

one little-known delegate and asked about the man's wife, who had been ill.

After endless debate, the PNC agreed to vote on making UN Resolution 242 the basis for future negotiations on Palestine. In other words, council members would have to vote whether to accept Israel's right to exist and live in peace with its neighbors.

Arafat's chief rival, George Habash, now partly paralyzed from a stroke, argued hotly against accepting Resolution 242. His ally, Nayef Hawatmeh, head of the Democratic Front for the Liberation of Palestine, backed him with a blizzard of amendments, trying to avoid a clear vote on Resolution 242. The turning point came when Salah Khalef, whom delegates knew as Abu Iyad, onetime head of Black September, made a passionate appeal for the delegates to accept the UN resolution. His influence turned the militant tide. Delegates finally voted 253 for, 46 against.

The PNC decision was a personal triumph for Arafat and his efforts to create unity within the PLO. The radicals agreed to stay in the PLO even after a vote that, in effect, recognized Israel. Habash declared that the PFLP still disagreed, but would go along rather than split the PLO. He warned that it was now up to the majority to convince the United States to use its influence with Israel to bring about negotiations. Syrian-based radicals, however, threatened to form their own PLO.

The National Council made another symbolic move. On November 15, it declared the independence of Palestine, and the formation of the new state. Later, the group also elected Arafat as interim president of Palestine until such time as a true state came into being in which elections could be held.

A month after the Algiers meeting, Arafat took two steps the United States had insisted upon and the PLO had resisted for thirteen years. At a UN meeting in Geneva, he accepted the idea of two states—a Palestinian state and a Jewish state, Israel, in Palestine. Arafat also said the PLO renounced terrorism.

The United States promptly agreed to end its thirteen-year boycott of the PLO, and to meet with PLO representatives to begin a new peace process. Hopes did not look particularly bright, however. Prime Minister Shamir of Israel mocked the Geneva announcement as a "monumental lie," and said Arafat's recognition of Israel was a "diabolical scheme" to destroy Israel by stages. He said Jordan was still the only legitimate partner for negotiations.

Together, the Intifada and the PLO shifts served to deepen Israeli fears of a violence-prone Palestinian state on its doorstep. Israelis of all political leanings feared that such a state would never live in peace with Israel. Thus the PLO and Israel entered the 1990s with a new set of political realities.

CHAPTER 9

THE PLO IN THE 1990s

After taking two giant and risky steps for an Arab—
recognizing Israel and renouncing terrorism—Arafat
waited for a dramatic response. He expected the United
States to step in and arrange talks between Israel and
the PLO, talks that might lead to Israeli withdrawal from
the West Bank and Gaza.

Arafat realized that he and other Arabs had ignored
many earlier chances to make peace, and that every
missed opportunity left Palestinians worse off. Israel's
former foreign minister, Abba Eban, once joked that the
PLO never missed an opportunity to miss an opportunity. As Arafat now admitted, "We have missed too
many opportunities in the past. We cannot afford to lose
this one."[1]

In 1948, Arabs missed the chance to create a Palestinian state because they tried to prevent the creation of
a Jewish state. In 1967, Arab nations and the PLO turned
down an Israeli offer to trade land for peace. By 1990,
the PLO—or at least that part of the PLO controlled by
Arafat—was trying to trade peace for land. Arafat said

the organization was willing to make a deal with Israel.

In response, however, Israel said it didn't trust Arafat and wouldn't deal with a bunch of terrorists, the PLO. Nor was Israel alone in suspecting PLO promises. Many observers questioned whether the PLO could be trusted to keep its word, or whether it would go right on trying to erase Israel from the map, despite talk of peace. They questioned Arafat's grip on the organization, and his ability to stop Palestinian terrorism. B'nai B'rith, a major American Jewish organization, took a full-page newspaper ad raising just such questions. "Why is Arafat silent when member groups of the PLO send terrorists into Israel? If he cannot stop them, does he speak for the PLO?"[2]

Such questions surrounded the PLO of the 1990s. Yet efforts to bring Israel to the negotiating table were only one of the PLO's concerns. Less than 40 percent of the approximately 5 million Palestinians the PLO represented lived in the West Bank and Gaza, where Arafat said he hoped to create the state of Palestine. What happened to other Palestinians? Some 2.3 million Palestinians lived in Syria, Jordan, Lebanon, and other Arab states. About 800,000 of them were in refugee camps. The largest group, more than 1.3 million, lived in Jordan, representing more than half of Jordan's total population.

Would people whose families came from places that were now permanent parts of Israel—Jerusalem, Haifa, Jaffa, for instance—be content with a Palestine that was only the West Bank or the Gaza Strip? Most of the PLO fedayeen came from Galilee and the coastal area that was now part of Israel. Would they remain loyal to a PLO that settled for just the West Bank and Gaza instead of fighting to regain their old homes? Israelis doubted it.

In Lebanon, hundreds of thousands of Palestinians

lived in constant danger from warring Lebanese factions and quarreling Palestine guerrilla forces. When fighting between two Muslim radical groups (one backed by Iran, one by Syria) threatened camps in Sidon in 1990, Fatah moved 1,000 troops into position around the refugee camps. A few days later, Israeli jets attacked the PLO positions. Later that same year, in a three-day battle, Fatah forces drove Palestinian followers of Abu Nidal from the Lebanese refugee district in southern Lebanon. The PLO, in other words, was still fighting shooting wars.

Yet having made a bold move toward peace, Arafat turned his restless energies to finding a way to get a peace process started. His goal was an international peace conference under United States sponsorship. However, Arafat's hopes for peace very quickly ran aground on the twin rocks of Israeli politics and Palestinian terrorism.

ISRAEL'S REACTIONS

At the heart of the Palestinian dilemma is Israel's need for security and the refusal of the Arab world to accept the fact that Israel exists. Every Arab state except Egypt is still technically at war with Israel. A tiny nation surrounded by more than 160 million hostile Arabs, Israel will take no action that might jeopardize the nation's safety. Nor will the United States, Israel's strongest ally, ask Israel to do so. Israelis tend to doubt Arab promises, particularly Arafat's. Prime Minister Yitzhak Shamir put the distrust in its most extreme form: "For us Arafat is like Hitler. He wants to see every one of us dead."[3]

Even Israelis with more flexible views share a sense of living under permanent siege. Every Israeli child is taught never to pick up a package or bag left lying in a public place; it might be a bomb planted by Palestinians. Israelis have had to fight five wars to defend their small country from surrounding Arabs. They point out that Arabs can afford to lose a war, since they have many Arab lands into which to retreat. Israelis cannot afford to lose a war. Losing a war would mean the loss of the state of Israel. It would mean the end of a Jewish state where any Jew can find a home and safety. No Israeli politican, no matter how eager for peace, would risk such a situation.

Most Israelis do not believe that the PLO has in fact given up its long-standing plan to eliminate Israel. After hearing for more than forty years that Palestinians want the land that is now Israel back, Israelis simply do not believe PLO promises. "The PLO has to convince the Israelis that after threatening them with murder and extinction for decades, it has now really changed its mind," [4] said a Jerusalem political science professor, Shlomo Avineri. He added that it was not enough for the PLO to convince the outside world it had given up trying to destroy Israel; it also has to prove it to skeptical Israelis.

Five months after Arafat's December 1988 announcements, a poll showed that an overwhelming majority of Israeli Jews opposed negotiating with the PLO. However, they said they would favor talks later if the PLO showed it had become more moderate. Nearly two thirds said they thought talks with the PLO were inevitable in the next five years. [5] Later polls showed similar results, reflecting deep Israeli suspicion of the PLO.

The fact that Israel is governed by a shaky coalition makes it harder to take the first steps toward peace talks. Shamir's Likud party does not have a majority in the Israeli parliament. To gain enough votes to form a government, Likud must make deals with the other sixteen political parties represented. Small hard-line parties are determined not to negotiate with the PLO. One coalition government broke up in 1989 over the issue of beginning a peace process. When a new coalition finally emerged in 1990, Shamir's margin of votes was far too tiny to take any bold steps toward peace.

The official Israeli reason for refusing to talk to the PLO has been the organization's history of terrorism. There may be another reason as well. "The present Israeli government fears that talking to the PLO goes a long way toward accepting the legitimacy of Palestinian aspirations for a state that would constitute a mortal danger for Israel," wrote Middle East expert Gideon Gottlieb in a 1989 issue of *Foreign Affairs*. He added, however, that there is wide agreement that Israel should no longer rule over the West Bank and Gaza. The Shamir government, of course, disagrees, and in fact encourages Jewish settlement in the occupied territory, a policy that inflames Palestinians.

THE WEST BANK, JUDEA, AND SAMARIA

Prime Minister Shamir speaks not of the West Bank, but of Judea and Samaria, the Biblical names for the area. To Shamir, Judea and Samaria are part of "greater Israel." The Likud party he heads has urged Jewish Israelis to move to Judea and Samaria, and offers low-cost housing and loans to encourage settlement. By 1990, some 80,000 Israelis lived in 140 settlements amid the 800,000 Palestinians in the West Bank and the Gaza Strip. The mix was explosive even before Shamir signaled plans to move many more settlers into the West Bank. In 1990 he noted that Israel expected tens of thousands of Jewish immigrants from the Soviet Union (which had just given permission for many Jews to leave). A "big Israel" would be needed to make room for the newcomers, said Shamir. A "big Israel" includes the West Bank.

Israel's other major political party, Labor, favors

trading the occupied territories for a binding peace treaty with Arab states. Labor also opposes more Jewish settlement in the West Bank (as do some members of Likud). The United States has urged Israel to end its occupation, and to begin peace discussions. Yet all are wary of negotiating with the PLO, and deeply cautious about accepting as sincere Arafat's statements about abandoning terrorism or about admitting that Israel has a right to exist in peace.

CAN ARAFAT AND THE PLO BE TRUSTED?

Many Israelis speak Arabic as well as Hebrew and English. They say that before anyone accepts Arafat's statements at face value, people should note what he and other PLO spokesmen say in Arabic to Arab audiences. PLO leaders have told Arab audiences that their peace offensive is part of a phased plan to destroy Israel. After the Palestinian parliament recognized Israel, the chairman of the PNC, Sheik Abdel Hamid Sayeh, was quoted as saying, "We want the whole of Palestine."

A Kuwaiti newspaper quoted Abu Iyad as saying, "We shall liberate Palestine stage by stage. The borders of the [Palestine] state as we declare it represent only part of our national aspirations. We shall work to expand them in order to realize our aspirations for all of the land of Palestine." Such statements would seem to indicate that talking peace may be only a ploy, not an honest offer to make a deal. Yet in a videotaped address smuggled into Israel and presented at a peace symposium in 1989 (no PLO person is allowed in Israel), Abu Iyad asked, "Does any Israeli really believe it is possible to destroy the five million Palestinians? We have concluded that we cannot destroy the Israeli people."

■ 146

Which statement is the truth? Has the PLO at long last become realistic, or do its leaders still cherish wild dreams of death and destruction for Israel?

Many Israelis argue that a Palestinian state on their doorstep would be a launching pad for destroying Israel. The warlike statements in Arabic prove that the PLO does not truly want peace, they say, and calls for peace are only a tactic, not an honest offer to negotiate a solution in good faith.

In response, PLO leaders ask for understanding of how great a leap it is for Palestinians to accept the reality that they can never go back to the places where they were born. Arafat offered to sign a binding peace treaty with tough international controls to ensure that it is kept. In an interview on American television, he said he was willing to have the United Nations or the superpowers (the United States and the Soviet Union) guarantee any agreement.

Israelis are quick to point out that while the PNC said it renounced terrorism and recognized Israel, it did not rewrite the PLO charter. Article 19 still says that the "partition of Palestine in 1947 and the establishment of the state of Israel are entirely illegal, regardless of the passage of time, because they were contrary to the will of the Palestinian people and to their natural right in their homeland. . . ."

Arafat did not actually say in his UN speech that the PLO recognized Israel's right to exist. He said the PLO would seek a comprehensive settlement among the parties concerned in the Arab-Israeli conflict, including the state of Palestine, Israel, and other neighbors. Pressed the next day by reporters to say clearly that Israel could live in peace, he said that all parties in the conflict have the right to "exist in peace and security, including the state of Palestine, Israel, and their neighbors." He added, "I repeat for the record that we totally and absolutely renounce all forms of terrorism, including individual, group and state terrorism."

While visiting France in 1989, Arafat was again questioned about Article 19. He replied that the PLO charter calling for the destruction of Israel was *caduc,* a French word that means obsolete or null and void. When the PNC declared the formation of a Palestinian state in 1988, said Arafat, it made the charter obsolete. "The declaration of independence is founded on a two-state solution and the charter is *caduc.*" As far as Arafat is concerned, therefore, the PLO had met the conditions set by the U.S. government before it would agree to press Israel to hold peace talks. Others disagreed, and asked why the governing body of the PLO did not meet to change the covenant, if indeed the PLO was no longer pledged to destroy Israel. Unless the covenant is formally changed, they say, why should Israel trust Arafat's promises?

IS PEACE POSSIBLE?

Is there any way out of the maze of anger, distrust, and competing and passionate claims to Palestine? Any effort to solve the Palestinian problem must deal with an explosive set of issues. As former United States Secretary of State Henry Kissinger once summed up: What territories, if any, will Israel give up? Who shall govern there? What security arrangements will prevail after Israel withdraws? Can Israel be asked at the same time to give up territories and allow the foundation of a PLO state?[6]

Arafat hoped after his December 1988 announcements that the United States would press Israel to meet with the PLO to work out a settlement. A few months later, he felt that he had conceded much and Israel nothing at all. "We have accepted two states in Palestine, and when we say that, who else could we mean but Israel and Palestine?''[7] He told an interviewer that he is challenging Israel to peace, and that he does not ask to be trusted; he asks to be tested.[8]

Israel for the most part ignored Arafat's overtures. Instead, the Israelis suggested a process for settling the issue of the West Bank and Gaza without PLO involvement. Prime Minister Shamir agreed to hold talks about the occupied territories, but wanted to set the rules for who could negotiate for the Palestinians. The Shamir plan called for elections in the West Bank and Gaza, under Israeli supervision, to choose the negotiators. However, no one linked with the PLO would have been allowed to be a candidate. Shamir also insisted that elections be held only after the Intifada ended.

Both the United States and Egypt tried to get talks started, but had little success. In May 1989, Secretary of State James Baker told an American Jewish audience that Israel must ''lay aside, once and for all, the unrealistic vision of a greater Israel.'' He urged Israel to stop Jewish settlement in the occupied territories, and to move toward negotiations for peace. He also said the PLO should amend its charter and renounce its long-standing phased plan to take over Israel.

Since Egypt is the only Arab state that has diplomatic relations with Israel, President Hosni Mubarak tried to act as a mediator. Working closely with the United States, Mubarak proposed his own plan in 1989, and suggested that talks be held in Egypt. The sticking point in all of these ideas became Israel's refusal to talk to any PLO representative, and the PLO's insistence (backed by Arab states) that the PLO speaks for the Palestinian people.

Despite almost total lack of progress, some ideas for solutions have gained support. Many people suggest some kind of confederation, or loose political linkage, between Jordan and whatever Palestinian state or entity is created. Arafat notes that 1.35 million Palestinians live in Jordan; he therefore thinks a confederation makes sense. No one knows what form such a confederation might take, but Israel has not ruled out this particular idea. Most doubt that it would be a full-scale national state, because Israel probably would not agree to that. Some sort of a mini-state seems more acceptable.

Arafat has even talked of a three- or four-sided economic union of Palestine, Jordan, Israel, and possibly of Lebanon. Such an idea seems unthinkable today, given the simmering hatreds aboil in the region. Arafat argues that Europeans fought each other for centuries, but today the youth of Europe live peacefully together instead of killing each other as their fathers did. Why could not the same thing happen in Palestine and Israel? Former U.S. secretary of state George Shultz wrote in 1990 that some form of confederation between Israel, the Palestinians, Jordan, and perhaps Egypt seems both necessary and inevitable.[9] By fall of 1990, however, all such talks of a permanent solution had been forgotten, and Arafat was once again waist-deep in controversy. His promises were not believed, and the PLO had lost most of the goodwill his peace efforts had built up.

CAN HE CONTROL THE TERRORISTS?

On the same day that Arafat said the PLO charter was *caduc,* one of his senior aides was shot in the head by a masked gunman in Beirut. It was the second terrorist attack on a PLO official in a week. The attacks showed once again that Arafat may have given up terrorism, but Palestinian radicals have not.

The U.S. State Department, which tracked PLO actions after the December 1988 announcements, said several months later that Arafat for the most part had, up to that time, kept his word not to use terrorism. However, such promises do not bind terrorists like Abu Nidal, who don't want peace with Israel, and who continued to stalk both PLO leaders and Israelis.

Some PLO units also continued hit-and-run raids in Israel after the 1988 announcement, though Fatah stopped raiding for several months. Arafat felt that he had kept his word. Accused of reneging on his promise not to use terror, he insisted that people should distinguish between terrorism as a crime and the "just national struggle against occupation." [10] He argued that Palestinians, as a people under army occupation, have a right to resist. Yet to Israelis, PLO raids on civilian targets are terrorism pure and simple.

Every act of terrorism, whether by the PLO or other Palestinians, stiffened the Israeli government's determination not to deal with the PLO. In July 1989, a twenty-eight-year-old Palestinian on a commuter bus from Tel Aviv to Jerusalem suddenly grabbed the steering wheel, shouted "Allahu Akbar" (God is Great), and sent the bus hurtling into a 400-foot rocky ravine, where it burst into flames. Fourteen people died and twenty-nine more were hurt, including the Palestinian. An Islamic group, Islamic Holy War, claimed responsibility and called the bus crash a heroic operation. It was one of several suicide terrorist attacks staged in the last few years by Islamic fundamentalists. The crash of bus #405 inside Israel itself sharpened Israeli rage and suspicions of Arabs in general.

Nayef Hawatmeh's Democratic Front for the Liberation of Palestine, which is part of the PLO, refused to accept Arafat's statement renouncing terror. DFLP commandos continued to raid into Galilee from Lebanon, though Israeli security forces caught most of the commandos before they reached their targets.

Another uproar followed Arafat's reported remark that any Palestinian who opposed the Intifada "exposes himself to the bullets of his own people."[11] Israelis say the comment was a threat, a way of bullying those who didn't go along with the PLO. Arafat insisted he was simply expressing reality, that passions were so high in the occupied territories that people opposed to the uprising became the targets of assassins. The U.S. State Department released a tape of Arafat's comments in Arabic. The translation read, "Whoever thinks of stopping the Intifida before it achieves its goals, I will give him ten bullets in the chest."[12]

The question of whether Arafat can be trusted is particularly important to the United States because the United States opened direct talks with him after assurances from President Mubarak of Egypt, King Fahd of Saudi Arabia, and other Arab leaders that Arafat could be trusted to keep his word on the conditions set for any possible peace talks.

That fragile trust shattered in May 1990, when Israeli security forces intercepted boats of terrorists from the Palestine Liberation Front as they landed on a crowded Israeli beach. The attack, in a popular recreation spot, sent shock waves through Israel, and drew harsh demands that all contact with the PLO be dropped. Abul Abbas, who heads the PLF, sits on the PLO executive committee. The U.S. government demanded that Arafat formally condemn the raid and insisted that he take action to remove Abbas from the PLO executive committee. Though four Palestinians were killed and eleven arrested, the raid may have achieved Abbas's real goal— to sabotage Arafat's efforts to get peace talks under way.

When Arafat did not promptly and totally condemn the raid, many Americans who had favored trying to work with the PLO said they were no longer as willing to do so. President Bush finally broke off the low-level talks with the PLO. Once again, terrorists had prevented even small steps toward settling the Palestine issue and achieving some sort of peace in the Middle East.

SIDING WITH SADDAM HUSSEIN

Any real momentum for peace talks had already sputtered out by the time Iraq's invasion of Kuwait canceled all chances of a quick settlement. On August 2, 1990, Saddam Hussein's armies rolled across the borders of the immensely rich but thinly populated kingdom of Kuwait. Within a day, Iraq controlled Kuwait and its enormous pools of oil. The Iraqi takeover set off a political earthquake in the Middle East, reshuffling loyalties, alliances, power, and money. Old patterns vanished almost overnight.

Despite the fact that Kuwait's royal family had bankrolled the PLO for more than twenty years, Arafat promptly praised the invasion. Arab telecasts showed him in Baghdad, Iraq's capital, grinning in the jubilant embrace of the Iraqi president. The PLO news agency WAFA sent a message to Palestinians in the West Bank and Gaza quoting Arafat: "We can only be in the camp hostile to Israel and its imperialist allies, who have mobilized all their sophisticated war machine not to come to anybody's aid but to protect their own interests."

That one sentence undid "years of his own energetic diplomacy," noted the respected *New York Times* foreign affairs columnist Flora Lewis. "So much for the peace initiative, the desire for negotiations, the recognition of Israel."[13]

Acting with rare speed and directness, an Arab summit meeting voted 12–3 to condemn the Iraqi invasion and to send a joint Arab military force to defend Saudi Arabia against possible attack by Iraq. Only Libya, Jordan, and the PLO voted against the move to send Arab

The PLO chairman met with Iraqi president Saddam Hussein on August 5, 1990, just days after Iraq invaded and occupied Kuwait.

troops to join U.S. and other forces rushing to defend Saudi Arabia. At least that was the vote announced after the closed session meeting. The vote, plus his public praise of Hussein, triggered a fire-storm of criticism against Arafat and the PLO among outsiders—though many Palestinians agreed completely with the stand.

As criticism swirled around him, Arafat insisted that the PLO had not in fact voted against the Arab League resolution to send troops to defend Saudi Arabia. He claimed that the PLO had in fact abstained from voting. Arab League officials later confirmed this version of the events, but it was too late to undo the public damage caused by the earlier announcement of the ''no'' vote.

No matter how PLO spokesmen tried to mask the fact, many PLO leaders and PLO groups mobilized immediately to fight alongside the Iraqis against U.S. and other forces in the Gulf. Palestinian radicals and terrorists hurried to Baghdad to enroll in Hussein's crusade. Among them were many PLO figures. According to a report in the *Wall Street Journal,* every PLO guerrilla group, including Arafat's Fatah, had pledged to remove U.S. forces from Saudi Arabia. Terrorist Abu Abbas, a member of the PLO executive council, ordered his followers to ''open fire on the American enemy everywhere.'' [14]

However he may have voted at the Arab summit, Arafat did side enthusiastically with the Iraqi invader. In so doing, he was once again echoing the passionate emotions of the people he leads. Seething with hatreds and dreams of revenge over their condition as stateless people, Palestinians in the streets of Jordan, the West Bank, and Gaza greeted the Iraqi invasion with bursts of cheering.

When Hussein threatened to wipe out half of Israel with chemical weapons, the announcement set off celebrations in the West Bank, Gaza, and Jordan. In another move to win Arab sympathies, the Iraqi president offered to withdraw his armies from Kuwait if the Israelis would withdraw from the West Bank and Gaza. He therefore positioned himself to become a possible savior in the eyes of Palestinians. With Saddam Hussein suddenly the new idol of the poorest Palestinians, Arafat scrambled to seem more militant.

A second reason for Arafat's support of Iraq was his deepening gloom and despair over the reluctance of the United States to step up pressure on Israel to talk peace with the Palestinians. In the months before the Kuwait invasion, Arafat had edged slowly into a closer alliance with the radical leader of Iraq.

Many Western observers said Arafat's decision to tie himself to Saddam Hussein had cost Arafat all the momentum and goodwill gained by the Intifada, and made it impossible to talk of solving the Palestinian dilemma soon. Arafat's stand alienated Israel's small but vocal peace movement, which had been calling for serious peace talks with the PLO. And, while the decision to back Saddam Hussein played well in poorer Palestinian neighborhoods, it outraged many Arab leaders as well as the wealthy Palestinians who had donated money to the PLO for years. The rich Arab oil states hinted that the PLO might have seen the last of their money. A top PLO official told a reporter a few weeks after the invasion, "As long as Yasir Arafat is at the head of the organization, I suspect the Gulf countries will boycott us completely."[15] He did not have to add that a major share of the PLO's budget had been flowing from those oil-rich Gulf states.

While Arafat scrambled to reglue his tattered supports, his old rival George Habash came out squarely behind Iraq and ready to fight. The radical leader of the Popular Front for the Liberation of Palestine, the PLO's second-largest group, called for all Arabs to "resist the

American invasion of the Arab region and to defeat the aggressive forces'' of the West and the Arab world.[16] Habash underscored his ties with Iraq by uprooting the PFLP from Syria to Baghdad, capital of Iraq.

As the United States and its allies mobilized a vast military buildup in the Persian Gulf to block Iraq's ambitions, Arafat worked feverishly to stitch together a face-saving formula that would let Hussein back down and withdraw his troops. Arafat called for a UN peacekeeping force in Kuwait after Iraqi withdrawal, and linked this proposal with yet another call for international talks to settle the Israeli-Palestinian issue.

Despite such efforts, Arafat's public support for the Iraqi invasion damned him in the eyes of most world leaders. It confirmed the worst fears of Israelis and of the many Americans who question whether the PLO or Arafat can be trusted. A *Wall Street Journal* editorial called the ''experienced terrorists'' of the PLO potent weapons in Hussein's arsenal. ''This sends a clear message to the Americans who hoped the PLO had changed its stripes and to leaders of the Arab Gulf states who had convinced themselves that hush money would protect them. The PLO has shown that its cardinal rule remains: Always side with the most radical force in the Arab world.'' [17] For just such reasons, the editorial added, the PLO could not be trusted with the responsibility of running a state of its own.

Faced with critics on all sides, and the death of hopes for peace talks that might lead to a Palestinian state, PLO officials and news agencies issued a blizzard of statements, many of them contradictory. Bassam Abu Shariff, the PLO's official spokesman, was quoted in late August as saying, ''We cannot possibly support the usurpation [seizure] of one Arab country by another.'' [18] At the same time, PLO radicals organized to fight alongside Iraqi troops. The PLO, in other words, seemed hopelessly split, its leadership in open disagreement and disarray.

The Iraqi wild card sidelined Arafat's long-standing dream of gaining a homeland for the Palestinian people with himself as its head. It made Arafat's earlier talk of a three- or four-sided peace deal with Israel, Jordan, and Lebanon seem utterly unrealistic, at least in the near future.

WHAT ARAFAT HAS BUILT

Given more than forty years of hatred, war, and terrorism, Arafat's lifelong goal of a Palestinian state seemed only that—a dream. Yet the suggestion that the PLO would build a strong sense of national identity among Palestinians scattered over the world also seemed far-fetched when Arafat took over the organization in 1969. He has made the PLO an authentic voice for a scattered people. The PLO has represented not only the Palestinians living in the ancient land of Palestine. It also speaks for those people dispersed through the Middle East, and even for some who live in the United States. Most are not citizens of the countries where they live, since most Arab states will not give them citizenship. For these stateless people, the PLO has represented their hope to have a government of their own and a place of their own. In the meantime, the organization runs a network of social services that provides education, medical care, and cultural activities for Palestinians.

In *The Arabs: Journeys Beyond the Mirage*, journalist David Lamb wrote that while many Palestinians might question PLO tactics or Arafat's leadership, none would divorce himself from the organization spiritually. "It gave them, for the first time, an identity. It had fought for them, made the world aware of them, spoken for them when no one cared to listen." [19] He added that to deny the possibility of direct discussions with the PLO is also to deny the possibility of ever solving the Palestinian problem.

A political columnist for Israel's largest daily newspaper wrote before the Iraqi invasion of Kuwait that the "demonization" of Arafat was over. He said that instead of treating Arafat like the devil, Israelis were "asking themselves practical questions about whether he is the right person to deal with, whether he can deliver on his promises." [20] After the Iraq invasion, Israelis closed ranks, determined to have no dealings with the PLO or its leader.

Despite all these setbacks, Arafat refused to give up on his lifelong goal of a state for Palestinians. An optimist with seemingly unlimited energy, Arafat seems to believe that enough old hatred could be shelved to make a practical deal that would benefit both sides. He would like to be the person who brings about the peace that gives Palestinians a state of their own. He would like to be able to offer Palestinians passports and protections wherever they live, something they do not have as stateless people.

Newscaster Jim Lehrer reminded Arafat in a 1989 television interview that three Arabs in modern times had either negotiated with Israel or tried to negotiate with Israel: King Abdullah of Jordan, Anwar Sadat of Egypt, and Bashir Gamayal of Lebanon. "All three were assassinated by their fellow Arabs," he said. "Does that bother you?" [21] he asked.

Arafat's answer was no. He has lived with the risks of being a voice for change among Palestinians for many years. Asked by another interviewer in 1989 if he thought he could really end the conflict, Arafat said yes. However, he added, if he was wrong there was no problem; for the next Palestinian generation, "all the new leaders the Intifada is creating—will take up the task." [22]

APPENDIX

EXCERPTS FROM THE PALESTINIAN NATIONAL COVENANT

The following is the partial text of the Palestinian National Covenant, as published in English, by the PLO.

Articles of the Covenant

Article 1: Palestine is the homeland of the Arab Palestinian people; it is an indivisible part of the Arab homeland, and the Palestinian people are an integral part of the Arab nation.

Article 2: Palestine, with the boundaries it had during the British Mandate, is an indivisible territorial unit.

Article 3: The Palestinian people possess the legal right to their homeland and have the right to determine their destiny after achieving the liberation of their country in accordance with their wishes and entirely of their own accord and will.

Article 4: The Palestinian identity is a genuine, essential and inherent characteristic; it is transmitted from parents to children. The Zionist occupation and the dispersal of the Palestinian Arab people, through the disasters which befell them, do not make them lose their Palestinian identity and their membership of the Palestinian community, nor do they negate them.

Article 5: The Palestinians are those Arab nationals who, until 1947, normally resided in Palestine regardless of whether they were evicted from it or have stayed there. Anyone born, after that date, of a Palestinian father—whether inside Palestine or outside it—is also a Palestinian.

Article 6: The Jews who had normally resided in Palestine until the beginning of the Zionist invasion will be considered Palestinians.

Article 7: That there is a Palestinian community and that it has material, spiritual and historical connections with Palestine are indisputable facts. It is a national duty to bring up individual Palestinians in an Arab revolutionary manner. All means of information and education must be adopted in order to acquaint the Palestinian with his country in the most profound manner, both spiritual and material, that is possible. He must be prepared for the armed struggle and ready to sacrifice his wealth and his life in order to win back his homeland and bring about its liberation.

Article 8: The phase in their history, through which the Palestinian people are now living, is that of national struggle for the liberation of Palestine. Thus the conflicts among the Palestinian national forces are secondary, and should be ended for the sake of the basic conflict that exists between the forces of Zionism and of imperialism on the one hand, and the Palestinian Arab people on the other. On this basis the Palestinian masses, regardless of whether they are residing in the national homeland or in diaspora constitute—both their organization and the individuals—one national front working for the retrieval of Palestine and its liberation through armed struggle.

Article 9: Armed struggle is the only way to liberate Palestine. Thus it is the overall strategy, not merely a tactical phase. The Palestinian Arab people assert their absolute determination and firm resolution to continue their armed struggle and to work for an armed popular revolution for the liberation of their country and their return to it. They also assert their right to normal life in Palestine and to exercise their right to self-determination and sovereignty over it.

Article 10: Commando action constitutes the nucleus of the Palestinian popular liberation war. This requires its escalation, comprehensiveness and mobilization of all the Palestinian popular and educational efforts and their organization and involvement in the armed Palestinian revolution. It also requires the achieving of unity for the national struggle among the different groupings of the Palestinian people, and between the Palestinian people and the Arab masses so as to secure the continuation of the revolution, its escalation and victory.

Article 11: The Palestinians will have three mottoes: national unity, national mobilization and liberation.

Article 12: The Palestinian people believe in Arab unity. In order to contribute their share toward the attainment of that objective, however, they must, at the present stage of their struggle, safeguard their Palestinian identity and develop their consciousness of that identity, and oppose any plan that may dissolve or impair it.

Article 13: Arab unity and the liberation of Palestine are two complementary objectives, the attainment of either of which facilitates the attainment of the other. Thus, Arab unity leads to the liberation of Palestine; the liberation of Palestine leads to Arab unity; and work towards the realization of one objective proceeds side by side with work towards the realization of the other.

Article 14: The destiny of the Arab nation, and indeed Arab existence itself, depends upon the destiny of the Palestinian cause. From this interdependence springs the Arab nation's pursuit of, and striving for, the liberation of Palestine. The people of Palestine play the role of the vanguard in the realization of this sacred national goal.

Article 15: The liberation of Palestine, from an Arab viewpoint, is a national duty and it attempts to repel the Zionist and imperialist aggression against the Arab homeland, and aims at the elimination of Zionism in Palestine. Absolute responsibility for this falls upon the Arab nation—peoples and governments—with the Arab people of Palestine in the vanguard.

Accordingly the Arab nation must mobilize all its military, human, and moral and spiritual capabilities to participate actively with the Palestinian people in the liberation of Palestine.

It must, particularly in the phase of the armed Palestinian revolution, offer and furnish the Palestinian people with all possible help, and material and human support, and make available to them the means and opportunities that will enable them to continue to carry out their leading role in the armed revolution, until they liberate their homeland.

Article 19: The partition of Palestine in 1947 and the establishment of the State of Israel are entirely illegal, regardless of the passage of time, because they were contrary to the will of the Palestinian people and to their natural right in their homeland, and inconsistent with the principles embodied in the Charter of the United Nations, particularly the right to self-determination.

Article 20: The Balfour Declaration, the Mandate for Palestine and everything that has been based upon them, are deemed null and void. Claims of historical or religious ties of Jews with Palestine are incompatible with the facts of history and the true conception of what constitutes statehood. Judaism, being a religion, is not an independent nationality. Nor do Jews constitute a single nation with an identity of its own; they are citizens of the states to which they belong.

Article 21: The Arab Palestinian people, expressing themselves by the armed Palestinian revolution, reject all solutions which are substitutes for the total liberation of Palestine and reject all proposals aiming at the liquidation of the Palestinian problem, or its internationalization.

Article 22: Zionism is a political movement organically associated with international imperialism and antagonistic to all action for liberation and to progressive movements in the world. It is racist and fanatic in its nature, aggressive, expansionist and colonial in its aims, and fascist in its methods. Israel is the instrument of the Zionist movement, and a geographical base for world imperialism placed strategically in the midst of the Arab homeland to combat the hopes of the Arab nation for liberation, unity and progress. Israel is a constant source of threat *vis-à-vis* peace in the Middle East and the whole world. Since the liberation of Palestine will destroy the Zionist and imperialist presence and will contribute to the establishment of peace in the Middle East, the Palestinian people look for the support of all the progressive and peaceful forces and urge them all, irrespective of their affiliations and beliefs, to offer the Palestinian people all aid and support in their just struggle for the liberation of their homeland.

Article 23: The demands of security and peace, as well as the demands of right and justice, require all states to consider Zionism an illegitimate movement, to outlaw its existence, and to ban its operations, in order that friendly relations among peoples may be preserved, and the loyalty of citizens to their respective homelands safeguarded.

Article 26: The Palestine Liberation Organization, representative of the Palestinian revolutionary forces, is responsible for the Palestinian Arab people's movement in its struggle—to retrieve its homeland, liberate and return to it and exercise the right to self-determination in it—in all military, political and financial fields and also for whatever may be required by the Palestinian case on the inter-Arab and international levels.

Article 27: The Palestinian Liberation Organization shall co-operate with all Arab states, each according to its potentialities; and will adopt a neutral policy among them in the light of the requirements of the war of liberation; and on this basis it shall not interfere in the internal affairs of any Arab state.

Article 29: The Palestinian people possess the fundamental and genuine legal right to liberate and retrieve their homeland. The Palestinian people determine their attitude towards all states and forces on the basis of the stands they adopt *vis-à-vis* the Palestinian case and the extent of the support they offer to the Palestinian revolution to fulfil the aims of the Palestinian people.

Article 30: Fighters and carriers of arms in the war of liberation are the nucleus of the popular army which will be the protective force for the gains of the Palestinian Arab people.

Article 33: This Charter shall not be amended save by (vote of) a majority of two-thirds of the total membership of the National Congress of the Palestine Liberation Organization (taken) at a special session convened for that purpose.

From the *The PLO; the Rise and Fall of the Palestine Liberation Organization* by Jillian Becker, St. Martin's, 1984.

SOURCE NOTES

Introduction
1. Fawaz Turki, *Soul in Exile: Lives of a Palestinian Revolutionary* (New York: Monthly Review Press, 1988), p. 7.
2. *Vanity Fair* interview, February 1989.
3. Turki, p. 12.
4. *Interview,* December 1988.
5. Jimmy Carter, *The Blood of Abraham* (Boston: Houghton-Mifflin, 1986), p. 111.
6. Jillian Becker, *The PLO: The Rise and Fall of the Palestine Liberation Organization* (New York: St. Martin's, 1984), p. 5.
7. *Newsweek,* December 26, 1988.

Chapter 1
1. Thomas Kiernan, *Arafat: The Man and the Myth.* (New York: W. W. Norton, 1976), p. 67.
2. Alan Hart, *Arafat: Terrorist or Peacemaker?* (London: Sidgwick and Jackson, 1984), p. 77. (Written in cooperation with Arafat and the PLO.)
3. Turki, p. 15.
4. David K. Shipler, *Arab and Jew: Wounded Spirits in a Promised Land* (New York: Times Books, Random House, 1986), pp. 32–3.

5. Jonathan Dimbleby, *The Palestinians* (New York: Quartet Books, 1979), p. 88.

Chapter 2
1. Kiernan, p. 149.
2. *Vanity Fair,* February 1989, p. 115.
3. Kiernan, pp. 176–9.
4. Hart, pp. 90–1.
5. Ibid., p. 101.

Chapter 3
1. Dimbleby, p. 114.
2. Kiernan, p. 222.

Chapter 4
1. Kiernan, p. 258.
2. Hart, p. 281.
3. Pamela Ann Smith, *Palestine and the Palestinians (1876–1983)* (New York: St. Martin's, 1984), p. 195.
4. Avner Yaniv, *Dilemmas of Security: Politics, Strategy, and the Israeli Experience in Lebanon* (New York: Oxford University Press, 1987), p. 40.
5. Hart, p. 323.

Chapter 5
1. Helena Cobban, *The Palestine Liberation Organisation: People, Power and Politics* (Cambridge: Cambridge University Press, 1984), p. 54.
2. Albert Parry, *Terrorism: From Robespierre to Arafat* (New York: Vanguard, 1976), p. 50.
3. Dimbleby, p. 162.
4. Dan Bavly and Eliahu Salpeter, *Fire in Beirut: Israel's War in Lebanon with the PLO* (New York: Stein and Day, 1984), p. 25.
5. Becker, p. 108.
6. Shipler, p. 111.

Chapter 6
1. Becker, pp. 110–1.
2. Hart, p. 366.
3. Rashid Khalidi, *Under Siege: PLO Decisionmaking During the 1982 War* (New York: Columbia University Press, 1986), p. 29.

4. Cobban, p. 96.
5. Turki, p. 156.

Chapter 7
1. *New York Times,* November 28, 1989.
2. Rosemary Ruether and Radford Ruether, *The Wrath of Jonah: The Crisis of Religious Nationalism in the Israeli-Palestinian Conflict* (San Francisco: Harper and Row, 1989), p. 126.
3. *Interview,* December 1988.
4. *New York Review of Books,* June 11, 1987.

Chapter 8
1. *Foreign Affairs,* Summer 1988, pp. 964–66.
2. *New York Times,* March 15, 1989.
3. *New York Times,* April 29, 1989.
4. *Washington Post,* December 29, 1989.
5. *Washington Post* weekly edition, April 3–9, 1989.
6. *New York Times,* April 26, 1989. (Anthony Lewis column)
7. *New York Times,* October 19, 1989.

Chapter 9
1. *New York Times Magazine,* December 18, 1988, p. 39.
2. *New York Times,* April 14, 1989.
3. *Time,* April 25, 1988.
4. *New York Times,* Op Ed page, December 12, 1989.
5. *New York Times,* April 2, 1989.
6. *Foreign Affairs,* Fall 1989.
7. *New York Times Magazine,* December 18, 1988, p. 63.
8. *Vanity Fair,* February 1989, p. 113.
9. *Washington Post* weekly edition, March 12–18, 1990.
10. *New York Times,* May 2, 1989.
11. *New York Times,* January 8, 1989.
12. *New York Times,* January 19, 1989.
13. *New York Times,* September 5, 1990.
14. *Wall Street Journal,* editorial, August 31, 1990.
15. *New York Times,* August 14, 1990.
16. *Wall Street Journal,* editorial, August 31, 1990.
17. *Ibid.*
18. *New York Times,* September 4, 1990.
19. David Lamb, *The Arabs: Journeys Beyond the Mirage* (New York: Random House, 1987), p. 217.

20. *Washington Post* weekly edition, March 13–19, 1989, p. 17.
21. *New York Times,* May 1, 1989.
22. *Vanity Fair,* February 1989, p. 181.

FOR FURTHER READING

Bavly, Dan, and Eliahu Salpeter. *Fire in Beirut: Israel's War in Lebanon with the PLO*. New York: Stein and Day, 1984.

Becker, Jillian. *The PLO: The Rise and Fall of the Palestine Liberation Organization*. New York: St. Martin's, 1984.

Cobban, Helena. *The Palestine Liberation Organisation: People, Power and Politics*. Cambridge: Cambridge University Press, 1984.

Dimbleby, Jonathan. *The Palestinians*. New York: Quartet Books, 1979.

Hart, Alan. *Arafat: Terrorist or Peacemaker* (Written in cooperation with Arafat and the PLO). London: Sidgwick and Jackson, 1984.

Khalidi, Rashid. *Under Siege: PLO Decisionmaking During the 1982 War*. New York: Columbia University Press, 1986.

Kiernan, Thomas. *Arafat: The Man and the Myth*. New York: W. W. Norton, 1976.

Kimmens, Andrew C., ed. *The Palestine Problem*. Reference Shelf. New York: H. W. Wilson, 1989.

Lamb, David. *The Arabs: Journeys Beyond the Mirage.* New York: Random House, 1987.

McDowall, David. *The Palestinians.* New York: Gloucester, 1986.

Peretz, Don. *The Middle East Today.* 5th ed. New York: Praeger, 1988.

Ruether, Rosemary, and Radford Ruether. *The Wrath of Jonah: The Crisis of Religious Nationalism in the Israeli-Palestinian Conflict.* San Francisco: Harper and Row, 1989.

Shipler, David K. *Arab and Jew: Wounded Spirits in a Promised Land.* New York: Times Books, Random House, 1986.

Smith, Pamela Ann. *Palestine and the Palestinians (1876–1983).* New York: St. Martin's, 1984.

Stefoff, Rebecca. *Arafat.* New York: Chelsea House, 1988.

Stefoff, Rebecca. *West Bank/Gaza Strip.* New York: Chelsea House, 1988.

Turki, Fawaz. *Soul in Exile: Lives of a Palestinian Revolutionary.* New York: Monthly Review Press, 1988.

Yaari, Ehud. *Strike Terror: The Story of Fatah.* New York: Sabra Books, 1970.

Yodfat, Aryeh Y., and Yuval Arnon-Ohanna. *PLO: Strategy and Tactics.* New York: St. Martin's, 1981.

INDEX

N